Strategic Studies Institute
and
U.S. Army War College Press

SENIOR OFFICER TALENT MANAGEMENT:
FOSTERING INSTITUTIONAL ADAPTABILITY

Michael J. Colarusso
David S. Lyle

February 2014

The views expressed in this report are those of the authors and do not necessarily reflect the official policy or position of the Department of the Army, the Department of Defense, or the U.S. Government. Authors of Strategic Studies Institute (SSI) and U.S. Army War College (USAWC) Press publications enjoy full academic freedom, provided they do not disclose classified information, jeopardize operations security, or misrepresent official U.S. policy. Such academic freedom empowers them to offer new and sometimes controversial perspectives in the interest of furthering debate on key issues.

*****

CONTENTS

FOREWORD ix

1. Introduction 1

2. The Case for Change..11

3. Create a Flexible Talent Management
   Framework.. 33

4. Differentiate People... 47

5. Create Relevant Expertise
   with Individual Career Paths...........................81

6. Invest in Higher and Specialized
   Education...105

7. Improve Succession Planning..........................125

8. Provide Sufficient Assignment Tenure.......... 145

9. Prepare for Change.. 159

CONCLUSIONS — THE WAY AHEAD............ 169

BIBLIOGRAPHY..177

ABOUT THE AUTHORS......................................199

FOREWORD

Since 1983, the mission of the U.S. Army Office of Economic and Manpower Analysis (OEMA) has been to provide a sound basis for policy and planning for the Army of the future. Founded by General Maxwell Thurman, this Headquarters Department of the Army (HQDA) asset is nested within the U.S. Military Academy's Department of Social Sciences. The intellectual freedom and community-of-practice provided by this academic setting promotes out-of-the-box thinking, allowing OEMA analysts to devise solutions to strategic challenges facing not just the Army and the Department of Defense (DoD), but other government agencies as well.

In the last 4 years, OEMA has devoted a significant amount of its research to officer "talent management," systematic planning for the right number and type of officers to meet the Army's needs at **all** levels and at **all** times so that the majority of them are employed optimally. Despite a commissioned officer focus, many of OEMA's talent management principles generalize to any labor force, to include the other services, warrant officers, noncommissioned officers, and DoD civilians.

Officer talent management is a critical research area, as maximizing the unique contributions of each officer is vital to the Army's success in today's austere fiscal and manpower environment. More specifically, the Secretary of the Army, the Chairman of the Joint Chiefs, and the Army Chief of Staff are all focused upon creating an adaptable institutional Army, one that can rapidly respond to operational demands. To that end, this monograph analyzes current senior officer management policies and recommends ways to make that cohort more adaptable. A central finding is that all-ranks officer talent management is critical to creating adaptable senior leaders. While this monograph focuses upon officer personnel policy, follow-on research will tackle compensation policy and organizational redesign, also within a talent management framework.

DOUGLAS C. LOVELACE, JR.
Director
Strategic Studies Institute and
   U.S. Army War College Press

Under present conditions at home and abroad, it is obviously not enough . . . to provide good soldiers . . . and the leaders necessary to command them in battle. Today many of these leaders are called upon to work with foreign affairs experts, industrial managers, scientists, labor leaders, and educators. They participate in the drafting and promotion of legislation, in the preparation of a national budget, and in the determination of the American position on a wide variety of foreign policy issues. They are required to understand, to communicate with, and to evaluate the judgment of political leaders, officials of other executive agencies, and countless specialists. . . .[1]

> John Masland and Laurence Radway
> *Soldiers and Scholars*

ENDNOTE

1. John W. Masland and Lawrence I. Radway, *Soldiers and Scholars: Military Education and National Policy*, Princeton, NJ: Princeton University Press, 1957, p. vii.

SENIOR OFFICER TALENT MANAGEMENT: FOSTERING INSTITUTIONAL ADAPTABILITY

CHAPTER 1

INTRODUCTION

> If leadership depends purely on seniority you are defeated before you start.
>
> General George C. Marshall[1]

On September 1, 1936, George C. Marshall was commanding an infantry brigade in an interwar army of just 174,000 men, larger than Bulgaria's but smaller than Portugal's. Exactly 3 years later, he was appointed four-star general and Army Chief of Staff. In partnership with Secretary of War Henry L. Stimson, Marshall would lead the Department of the Army (its corporate or "institutional" headquarters) as it raised, trained, equipped, deployed, and in general ensured the readiness of U.S. land and air combat forces. With war clouds looming, the new chief felt ill-prepared for the task. Recollecting his first days on the job, Marshall said:

> It became clear to me that at the age of 58 I would have to learn new tricks that were not taught in military manuals . . . the arts of persuasion and guile. I must become an expert in a whole new set of skills.[2]

Fortunately for the nation, Franklin Roosevelt had a shrewd eye for the talent demanded by the times. Reaching 34 names down the rank list of senior generals, he chose Marshall over Major General Hugh Drum. A two-star since 1930, Drum had served in almost every top position in the Army but Chief of

Staff—popular wisdom held that he was a shoe-in for the job. General Marshall's selection sent a clear signal to the officer corps that times were changing. Marshall was not chosen for the **position**—he was selected for the **work**. In other words, Roosevelt did not focus upon whom he had at the most senior levels, but instead upon who could best preside over a 40-fold increase in the force.[3] The President clearly understood that shifts in strategy require shifts in leadership traits.

Very quickly, Marshall identified officer talent management as woefully insufficient in the interwar Army, particularly at the senior ranks. Commenting upon the crop of generals he inherited as Chief of Staff, he noted that:

> Many of them have their minds set in outmoded patterns, and can't change to meet the new conditions they may face. . . . I do not propose to send our . . . soldiers into action under commanders whose minds are no longer adaptable. . . .[4]

To replace them, Marshall discarded the Army's moribund officer seniority system and implemented deep succession planning. With congressional approval in 1940, he gained complete control over the promotion and retirement process, allowing him to advance the right officers for the future challenges that would confront the Army:

> I've looked over the colonels, the lieutenant colonels, and some of the majors of the Army. . . . I'm going to start shifting them into jobs of greater responsibility than those they hold now. . . . Those who stand up . . . will be pushed ahead. Those who fail are out at the first sign of faltering.[5]

Marshall followed through on his pledge. Performance during a rigorous series of Army field exercises in 1941 (culminating in the well-known Louisiana maneuvers) became his centerpiece tool for screening, vetting, and culling senior officer talent. Thirty-one of 42 Army corps and division commanders were relieved or retired in the immediate aftermath of the maneuvers, most of whom had previously received glowing efficiency reports.[6] An additional 20 of 27 division commanders were cashiered in 1942, replaced largely by men who were majors, lieutenant colonels, or colonels on the eve of the war.[7] Despite the rapid ascension of these relatively junior officers, who had little previous experience commanding large formations, the United States created a massive citizen army that performed in veteran fashion during World War II, stunning the British in general and Winston Churchill in particular:

> It remains to me a mystery . . . how the very small staffs which the United States kept during the years of peace were able . . . to find the leaders . . . not only [capable] of creating mighty armies . . . but of leading and guiding those armies upon a scale incomparably greater than anything that was prepared for. . . .[8]

That leadership success was fostered by two things. The first was the Army's interwar emphasis upon education. Between 1919 and 1941, officers routinely spent one-half to two-thirds of their careers as students or instructors at West Point, in Reserve Officer Training Corps (ROTC) detachments, in branch schools, or at Fort Leavenworth and Carlisle Barracks.[9] In fact, in

1920, the War Department established the following officer manning priorities for its organizations:
1. The Army Staff;
2. The Army War College faculty;
3. The Command and General Staff College faculty; and,
4. The "Line" (operational troop units).[10]

In a time of post-conflict drawdown, threat uncertainty, and fiscal austerity, the Army refused to compromise on officer education because these professionals would provide the nucleus of a mobilization army should war come again. As General John Pershing said, "In no other army is it so imperative that the officers of the permanent establishment be highly perfected specialists."[11] In spite of victory in the Great War and an officer corps heavy in combat experience, there was a pervasive sense that the Army had to be led by more accomplished professionals and that education was the key to victory. Future conflicts would be very different—there would be no room for amateurism.

Such educational emphasis contrasts starkly with officer management culture and policy in the Army today. In the post-global war on terror (GWOT) era, one also characterized by a drawdown, fiscal austerity, and an uncertain threat environment, the most prized officer attribute is combat experience. This is followed by operational troop unit assignments (valued well above institutional leadership assignments), with continuing officer education coming in dead last.

The second contributor to the officer corps' World War II success was the sweeping institutional adaptations General Marshall introduced in response to a dynamically changing national security environment, particularly in the realm of officer management.[12] Marshall:

- ended the Army's officer seniority system by fearlessly seeking and securing the legislative authority to do so;
- retired or reassigned nonperformers, regardless of connections or political patronage;
- created field grade talent pools (looking all the way down to majors for emerging general officer talent) and made conscious assignment decisions to help develop and evaluate those officers;
- recognized the low utility of inflated evaluation reports in making senior officer management decisions; and,
- differentiated people—understood that some officers possessed other than "field" command talent and made them expert advisors on Army and interagency staffs.[13]

In other words, to expunge what he referred to as the bureaucratic ". . . bunk, complications, and ponderosities"[14] of his day, General Marshall created a dynamic officer talent management system and fervently devoted himself to it.[15]

While the results of Marshall's efforts spoke for themselves, the 1947 Officer Personnel Act (OPA) nevertheless turned away from the officer management principles so integral to the Army's wartime success. OPA's overriding purpose was to ensure the Armed Forces, particularly the Army, never again went into battle with a "hump" of mid-career officers blocking the advancement of those better suited to the demands of modern warfare. The hump was the result of World War I, when a mass of Regular Army commissions were granted to fill wartime vacancies. As "regulars," these mid-career officers were protected from involuntary separation. Many of them stayed on active duty in the small post-war Army until mandatory retirement at age 64, stunting the upward flow of junior officers commissioned after them.

How big was the interwar hump? Pretty darned big. By July 1932, for example, 46.5 percent of all officers had received their Regular Army commissions between April 1917 and July 1920, to include every captain on active duty.[16] As a result, many men commissioned after 1920 remained lieutenants for **12 or more years**.[17] The only way to advance was upon the death, retirement, or dismissal of a more senior officer. Talent did not matter, and with the nation in the grips of the Great Depression, few mid-career officers opted to leave the service.

The hump was so large that it blocked not just promotion, but education as well. For example, before World War I, Fort Leavenworth routinely matriculated the vast majority of officers—attendance at the Command and General Staff College was largely universal.[18] After the war, however, the college could no longer admit most mid-career officers, and the curriculum was slashed from 2 years to 1 in a desperate yet inadequate attempt to increase throughput.[19] These developments were anathema to the interwar Army's educational aspirations.

To avoid a repeat of the hump after World War II, OPA shifted the entire defense establishment to an "up-or-out" officer development model that remains fundamentally unchanged today.[20] As a result, virtually all officers are managed not by talents but by a rigid, time-driven methodology, one aimed at identifying and selecting a small pool of leaders for successively higher levels of command.[21]

While OPA may have solved the mid-career hump problem, it created equally vexing personnel challenges for today's Army. Managing all officers with an eye to enhancing their competitiveness for promotion and command profoundly affects not only generals, but also those at all ranks below them. Management consultant Nicholas Jans has observed that in professional western armies, this approach creates an operationally focused, command-centric culture in which:

> . . . military officers see their *raison d'être* [solely] as 'command' and their professional identity [solely] as 'warrior.' Most expect to make their reputations as commanders and support the use of command performance as the central criterion for career advancement.[22]

Because advancement requires a "warrior" career profile, officers studiously avoid nonoperational assignments. These are universally regarded as hazardous to one's career, even though such assignments can develop the specialized expertise demanded by the majority of senior officer duty positions, which are predominately nonoperational. Jans' conclusions were echoed in the U.S. Army's 2006 *Review of Education, Training and Assignments for Leaders* (RETAL Study):

> . . . a culture exists in the Army in which officers aspire to the highest positions of responsibility by selecting narrow career paths at the expense of development in the skills needed in the non-kinetic spectrum. . . . Often times the current culture discourages experiences outside of the traditional career track.[23]

Unfortunately, a rigid, time-based, up-or-out system, while fairly simple from a management perspective, engenders talent flight and is devoid of the dynamic talent management which must be implemented across the entire officer corps to ensure senior officers are equal to future national security demands. As we will see, a growing number of voices both inside and outside of the Army are calling for change. This monograph articulates a theoretical framework for such change and also recommends several policy options.

ENDNOTES - INTRODUCTION

1. Marshall to the Truman Committee in 1941, available from *www.marshallfoundation.org/MarshallonLeadership.htm*.

2. Douglas T. Hall, *Careers In and Out of Organizations*, Thousand Oaks, CA: Sage Publications, Inc., 2002, p. 161.

3. In this regard, Franklin Roosevelt was not unlike his distant cousin, Theodore Roosevelt, who noted in his 1903 State of the Union address that "the only people who are contented with a system of promotion by mere seniority are those who are contented with the triumph of mediocrity over excellence."

4. Eric Larrabee, *Commander in Chief*, New York: Harper and Row, 1987, p.101.

5. *Ibid.*, pp. 101-102.

6. Marshall, of course, made missteps as a talent manager, often because he had to rely upon intuition or anecdote rather than hard information. Witness his assessment of Major General Lloyd Frendendall, a man he once considered as possible supreme commander of all U.S. forces in Europe until his standout failure as a corps commander during Operation TORCH in North Africa. Prior to that, Marshall had said, "I like that man; you can see determination all over his face." For a while, he also held back the eminently capable James van Fleet because he mistook him for a similarly named officer with a drinking problem.

7. Carlo D'Este, *Eisenhower: A Soldier's Life*, New York: Henry Holt and Co., 2002, pp. 279-280.

8. Larrabee, p. 120.

9. Marshall's own career was typical. For almost 9 consecutive years (1927-36) he taught at the U.S. Army War College, the Infantry School, or as a senior instructor with the Illinois National Guard.

10. Peter J. Schifferle, *America's School for War*, Lawrence, KS: University of Kansas Press, 2010, p. 90.

11. *Ibid.*, p. 19.

12. Bill Conaty, former General Electric Senior Vice President for Human Resources, could have been describing Marshall when talking about the critical talents organizations need in their leaders. These include the ability to ". . . make the right strategic bets, take calculated risks, conceive and execute new value-creating opportunities, and build and rebuild competitive advantage." See Conaty and Ram Charan, *The Talent Masters*. New York: Crown Business Press, 2010, p. 2.

13. General Lucius Clay is a notable example. A master logistician, he was made Deputy Director of the Office of War Mobilization and Reconversion (OWMR) under James Byrnes. As Clay put it, "This was not a job for an officer in wartime. I had no choice, though, and General Marshall quickly rejected my plea [for a combat command]."

14. Larrabee, p. 112.

15. Much like Marshall, today's most effective chief executive officers (CEOs) devote significant time to talent management. For example, GE's Jack Welch and his successor, Jeffrey Immelt, are well-known for spending 30-40 percent of their time on people issues, and GE's Senior Vice President for Human Resources is the second most influential person in the company. CEOs of other well-known "people factories" have done the same, to include A. G. Lafley of Proctor and Gamble and Bob Keegan of Goodyear. See Conaty and Charan, p. 264.

16. To get a sense of the problem, imagine that 35,000 of today's 77,000 Army officers were commissioned between 1998 and 2000. Then imagine allowing each to serve until age 64, regardless of rank, with no culling except for the most egregious of offenses. Career progression would grind to a halt, just as it did from 1920 to 1940.

17. Harry Richard Yarger, *Army Officer Personnel Management: the Creation of the Modern American System to 1939*, Doctoral dissertation, Temple University, 1986, pp. 213-214.

18. A staff study completed in 1937 showed that the vast majority of Regular Army colonels and lieutenant colonels (most of them commissioned before World War I), had attended the staff college. See Schifferle, pp. 132-134.

19. *Ibid.*, pp. 79-82.

20. Marshall and Eisenhower both supported the act. At the time, the Army's post-war officer management options were circumscribed by both the creation of the Department of Defense (DoD) and the lack of dynamic information technologies to provide relevant, accurate talent information.

21. For the most part, the 1980 Defense Officer Personnel Management Act (DOPMA) maintained the "up-or-out" system, which remains in place today. DOPMA does not mandate promotion timelines, but it does recommend them. While not law, they have become firmly entrenched within DoD's personnel management culture and policies. See Bernard Rostker *et al.*, *The Defense Officer Personnel Management Act of 1980: A Retrospective Assessment*, Arlington, VA: Rand Corporation, 1993, p. 13.

22. Nicholas Jans, "The 'Once Were Warriors' Syndrome and Strategic Leadership in the Profession of Arms," *CDCLMS Leadership Papers*, March 2004, p. 7. Jans is a retired brigadier general and Visiting Fellow at the Australian Defence College.

23. *U.S. Army RETAL Task Force, Officer Team Report*, June, 2006, p. 6.

CHAPTER 2

THE CASE FOR CHANGE

> The ability to make good decisions regarding people remains one of the last reliable sources of competitive advantage, since very few organizations are very good at it.[1]
>
> Peter Drucker

We have undertaken this examination of senior officer management practices because the last two Army Chiefs of Staff asked us to do so. As we began work, however, it became clear that any improvements in this area must be firmly rooted within a comprehensive, Army-wide evolution towards **all-ranks** officer talent management, one which provides both the structural and career flexibility needed to respond to whatever unanticipated crises the future may bring.

Our analysis takes place in a time of opportunity. After all, the U.S. Army remains the world's premier land force. Just as in George Marshall's day, however, that world is profoundly changing.[2] Today's "generalist" officer management approach may have been sufficient during the relative equilibrium of the Cold War era, with its industrial economies, planned mobilization of conscript armies, clear adversaries, and manageable pace of change, but it is unequal to the needs of a volunteer force facing the challenges of a competitive labor market, a relative decline in American economic power, and a complex global threat and operating environment that changes at breakneck pace. It is an approach requiring the Army to predict exactly which critical talents senior officers will need while simultaneously ensuring that each is "broad" enough to possess them all—an impossible task.

Before we go any further, some thoughts about the terms "generalist" and "broadening," which predominate in most discussions of officer corps management today. We believe that "generalist" is a misnomer. In reality, it refers to the Army's baseline—**land combat expert**. The Army produces land combat experts (as it must), noncombat experts (also as it must), and those rare few officers who are expert in multiple domains. When this is understood, the current fascination with "broadening" becomes clear—it means exposing land combat experts to the nonoperational world, usually for an inordinately brief time at mid-career or later. At best, it is an insufficient effort to develop expertise critical to the Army profession, particularly its institutional arm.

This management paradigm requires senior land combat experts to perform optimally in any assignment they receive yet rarely affords them the specialized education, development, or assignment tenure needed to succeed in the fundamentally different world of institutional leadership and management. Instead, it often forces them to draw upon talents developed during years of employment at the direct and organizational levels of leadership, some of which, even if honed to a razor's edge, are rapidly outmoded by today's accelerating pace of change. As one four-star general pointed out:

> From the time my grandfather, at the end of World War I, went from lieutenant to colonel, there was a change in technology. *But it was not so fast or so great that his experience did not provide him with a body of expertise that made him legitimate and credible with his men.* The reality today is when a general officer speaks to a captain, [he] has almost never used any of the communications equipment, intelligence assets, or weapons

systems that the captain has.... So the reality is: How does the leader retain his legitimacy? ... *Things go so fast now it's very difficult for people to be experts and still be leading.*[3]

Complicating things still further, the rapid job rotation of today's operationally focused career system makes adaptation a daunting task for even the brightest senior officers, particularly as they contend with strategic issues affecting the Army's future. Consider this: Up to brigade or division command, these dedicated professionals have had unit leadership extensively modeled for them. Before the first day on the job, for example, new company commanders have enjoyed years of company-level service as platoon leaders and perhaps as executive officers. They have been directly coached and mentored by seasoned company commanders, by their peers, and by noncommissioned officers alike. In short, they have been immersed in the world of company-level leadership. Because of this, their learning curves are flatter, and their command expertise is relevant and sufficient. Their familiarity with this environment makes them confident in their decisionmaking—they are not risk averse because they know which risks are prudent.[4]

The same holds true as these officers progress through troop leading assignments. As company commanders, they routinely interact with battalion commanders, executive officers, and operations officers. As battalion commanders, they imbibe deeply from the leadership modeled by their brigade commanders. As divisional staff officers or brigade commanders, they observe and work closely with division commanders and their assistant commanders. Granted, it is a fast-paced world in which leadership decisions can have life or death implications, but as a learning environment, it is a relatively comfortable and familiar one—these officers have been fully acculturated to the world of operational assignments. Whether an infantryman, tanker, engineer, intelligence analyst, or logistician, each officer knows how to orchestrate the contributions of his or her career field to battlefield victory—they're **all** land combat experts.

Now pluck an officer from this operational world (we will call him "Bob") and assign him for a year or so as the Army G1's Director of Military Personnel Management (or as the G3/5/7 Director of Force Management, the G8 Director of Integration, the G2 Director of Initiatives, etc.). Post Bob to the Pentagon, where he encounters the bifurcated civil-military staff structure for perhaps the first time and where more nuanced leadership in the form of consensus building, moral suasion, and interpersonal tact is required.[5] Provide him little or no overlap with his predecessor. Change out his boss at the halfway point, as well as half of his subordinates and peers across the Army staff (as Figure 2-1 shows, annual staff churn rates, particularly for senior officers, approach 50 percent). Lastly, inform Bob of his follow-on assignment 4 or 5 months prior to moving him there.

Regardless of how professional he is, under these circumstances, it is unlikely that Bob will exercise genuine strategic leadership—his **time span of discretion** prohibits it. Simply put, time span of discretion is the amount of time between taking an action and receiving feedback on its impact.[6] How can Bob build consensus, acquire and allocate resources, shape organizational culture, or grow the next generation of leaders in just over a year? Frankly, he cannot, and since he has only a few months to demonstrate accomplishments in an "up-or-out" system,

Share of Officers Who Departed the Organization in a Single Year (Average).

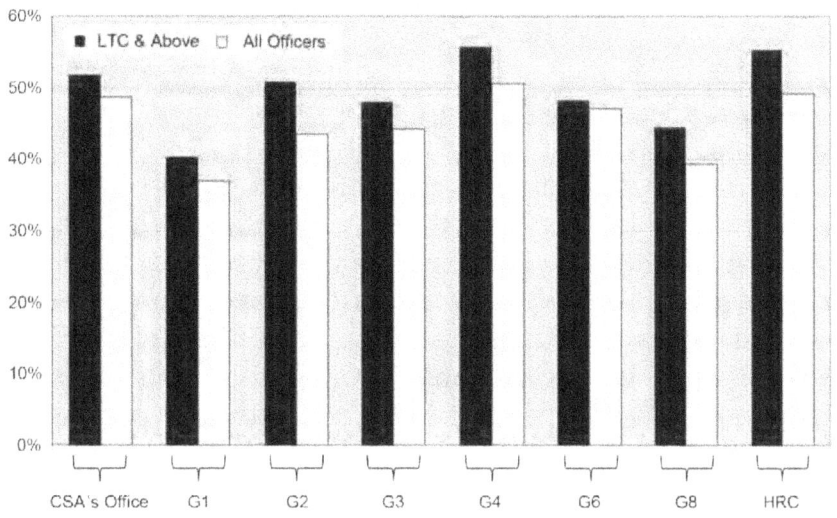

Source: U.S. Army Office of Economic and Manpower Analysis.

Figure 2-1. Average Annual Army Staff Section Churn (2005-11).

he will instead focus his efforts in areas of lesser significance, with correspondingly lower decision risk and higher likelihood of positive feedback.

Also consider that as a product of this system, Bob may lack the domain expertise needed to contend with the strategic issues of his office, hampering his innovation and creative risk taking. Even if he is appropriately expert for the job, Bob knows that any attempt at strategic decisionmaking may be undone by his successors during their equally short tenures. Finally, the short duration of Bob's assignment will cause him to look beyond it well before it ends. Why? Because he now works in a world where each new job demands talents which were never modeled for him. Because the Army has failed to do so, Bob must prepare himself for the future at the expense of the present. Quite understandably, he refuses to epitomize the "Peter Principle," which states that in a hierarchy, employees tend to be promoted until they reach a position at which they cannot succeed.[7]

As a result, many superbly talented senior officers are unable to lead institutional adaptation. While accomplished leaders, they're unable to provide change leadership.[8] Like the fireman on a steam locomotive, each stokes the bureaucratic engine but has little impact upon its destination.[9] It's a confounding situation, one in which the sum of the leadership parts is decidedly less than the whole. The Army must fix this in order to maintain its competitive advantage over potential adversaries, and three global challenges highlight the urgency of the situation.

CHALLENGE ONE: THE CHANGING ECONOMIC CLIMATE

While previous global downturns maintained or extended American economic dominance, current trends are diminishing U.S. economic power relative to that of several nations. Since 2000, the emerging economies of Brazil, India, China, and other countries have rapidly increased internal investment, enhancing their domestic productivity and giving rise to a more productive and educated middle class. Meanwhile, as the United States has continued its outsized defense spending (43 percent of the global total, roughly seven times that of China),[10] a third of its manufacturing jobs have disappeared, its middle class is shrinking, and increases in higher education have stalled.[11]

While the last decade of continuous warfare is not the source of U.S. economic woes, it has not helped. Total costs (including direct expenditures and macroeconomic impacts) are second only to those of World War II's inflation-adjusted $5 trillion.[12] Of course, total defense spending in this time frame amounts to just 6.2 percent of the gross domestic product (GDP), a far cry from the 37.8 percent of World War II.[13] Still, there have been significant collateral economic consequences.

First, the war has diverted investment from education, infrastructure, and research that would have made the United States far more productive in the long run. This is problematic, as victory in world affairs generally comes to those nations with a flourishing economic base. Second, it has been financed with deficits. As was the case with post-World War II Britain (which finally repaid its wartime debt to the United States in 2006), this debt may shift the United States closer to the second tier of economic powers. Finally, higher oil prices, in part a consequence of the war, have weakened the American economy.[14]

As a result of these economic trends, the Army now faces tremendous resource challenges. These include declining defense budgets over the next decade, with particularly deep cuts anticipated over the next 5 years. Those cuts will include a significant force drawdown. In this environment, talent management, particularly at the senior officer levels, is critical to successfully accomplishing more with less.[15]

CHALLENGE TWO: THE CHANGING NATURE OF WORK

In the Information Age, jobs are becoming more complex, requiring employees who are adaptive, inventive, and empathetic. "Knowledge economy" work is characterized by high levels of task interdependence, skill specificity, and rapid technological change. As a result, officers will increasingly find themselves using (and collaborating with) smart machines, not just in combat but also in training, education, intelligence, security, engineering, communications, and all other domains.

Human work processes will change as a result, necessitating new talents. Those talents will in many ways be quite different from those sought in productive people today. Sense-making, social intelligence, computational and adaptive thinking, cross-cultural fluency, new media literacy, interdisciplinary acumen, a design mindset, and the abilities to parse large volumes of information and collaborate virtually are just some of the skills senior officers will have to possess to varying extents.[16]

For example, the speed of Information Age change is rapidly outpacing the Army's planning, budgeting, and acquisition systems. As the Army Directed Studies Office notes:

> The Program Objective Memorandum (POM) cycle covers funding for programs nine years in the future. ... [Meanwhile], the Joint Capabilities Integration & Development System Process, combined with the Acquisition Process, results in a 7 to 14-year effort. This presents a case in which requirement documents written today *result in items being produced years into the future that will not be technologically current.*[17]

Just as they always have, these stifling bureaucratic procedures place a premium on change-embracing, prudent risk-taking officers. Consider the difference one such officer made to a procurement proposal languishing in the Ordnance Department in 1940:

> Major Walter Bedell Smith came in to interrupt a meeting [General] Marshall was having with some generals. In a minute . . . he described the plight of a salesman in his office who had been given the runaround everywhere else. . . . His company had designed a small, compact, lightweight vehicle with low silhouette that would carry four or five men and could be manhandled out of mud holes by its passengers. . . . "Well, what do you think of it?" asked Marshall. "I think it is good." Smith replied. "Well," said Marshall, "do it." Thus did the lowly jeep . . . enter the U.S. Army and its place in history as the most practical, adaptable, and everywhere beloved means of transportation the war produced.[18]

CHALLENGE THREE: THE CHANGING THREAT—FROM KINETIC TO ECONOMIC AND ASYMMETRIC

The U.S. share of global wealth and production has been steadily shrinking since the 1960s, a trend that is accelerating in this century. As a result, America is increasingly vulnerable to foreign powers seeking to enlarge their economic influence at its expense by manipulating currencies, commodities prices, and balances of trade. Several nations also seem willing to attack the U.S. economy directly, particularly with cyber weapons. In fact, the last two directors of national intelligence characterized cyber attack as the greatest threat to American security, and the prescience of their claims is supported by growing evidence.[19]

China, for example, is systematically hacking the computer networks of the U.S. Government and American corporations. According to Richard Clarke in the *Wall Street Journal*, "In a global competition among knowledge-based economies, Chinese cyber-operations are eroding America's advantage." More ominously, in 2009, the *Journal* also reported that the control systems for the U.S. electric power grid had been hacked, perhaps allowing the attacker to get back in at will.[20] This shows the relative ease with which an adversary could counter American military superiority by curtailing U.S. productivity and organization at home via asymmetric attack capabilities resulting from years of technology research and investment.

This emerging threat cannot be underestimated, for it adds a game-changing dimension to warfare, much as aviation did a century ago. Consider that in 1918, Brigadier General Billy Mitchell was as good a strategic air power innovator as any in the world. In 1945, General "Hap" Arnold could claim the same. But what is the Army doing today to cultivate its 21st century **cyber** counterparts, men and women who are already in its talent pipeline? More importantly, will these young innovators remain on the leadership periphery, or will the Army let them rise to the top of the institution as times dictate?

That was a question on the mind of Lieutenant General Rhett Hernandez, the first commanding general of Army Cyber Command, who sounded a lot like George Marshall when he said, "My job demands a whole range of talents that I may not yet possess." Meanwhile, he noted that two lieutenants on temporary duty at his headquarters, recent undergraduates with degrees in the computer sciences, "ran circles around the rest of the command." In the general's view, current, relevant domain expertise in this rapidly evolving field often trumps the legacy experiences of more senior officers and may even require a flatter, more collaborative organization rather than a deeply hierarchical one. His experience highlights that emerging technologies are particularly demanding of both new senior officer talents and the institutional adaptability required to unleash them.[21]

CHALLENGES RECOGNIZED BUT UNMET

For the better part of 2 decades, government and military leaders have voiced concern over the implications of these complex challenges for senior officer management. As early as 1997, Congress noted that the process for selecting, assigning, and developing general and flag officers "may not effectively prepare them for [the] increasing levels of responsibility" they will hold in a more challenging and complex future.[22] A particular concern was the rapid rate at which general and flag officers rotate through senior leadership positions (insufficient assignment tenure) and the impact of this upon organizational and individual effetiveness.

In 2001, the Government Accountability Office (GAO) characterized strategic human capital management as a "government-wide high risk area" and called for improved key leader succession planning and better human capital data systems to help differentiate people.[23] Nine years later, a 2010 House Armed Services Committee report concluded that senior officers serving in joint and service staff assignments lacked "adequate educational preparation."[24] Figure 2-2 helps illustrate that concern. Over the last 15 years, general officers have increasingly been a product of Professional Military Education (PME) schools only.

In 1995, for example, roughly 55 percent of brigadier generals possessed an in-resident graduate degree from a full-time civilian college or university. By 2010, however, that percentage had dropped by more than a third, a fundamental shift from past practices that some fear reflects a rising anti-intellectualism in the Army officer corps (we will examine this further in Chapter 6).

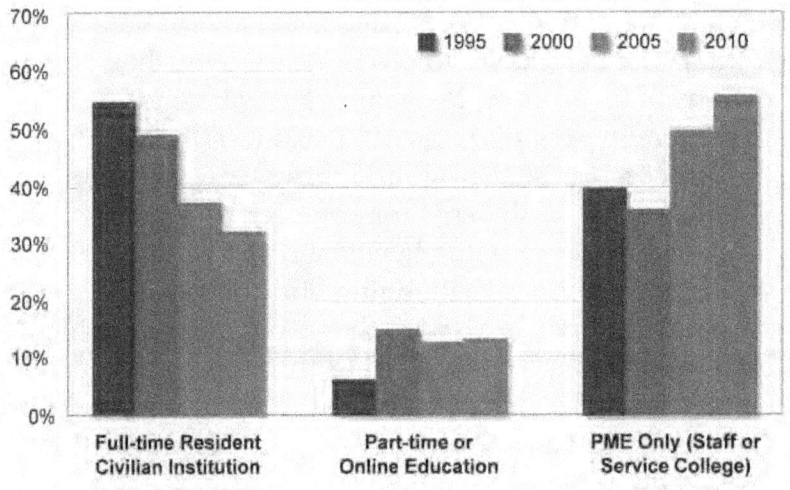

Source: U.S. Army Office of Economic and Manpower Analysis.

Figure 2-2. Brigadier General Cohort by Graduate Degree Type.

In parallel with congressional and GAO analyses, the Department of Defense (DoD) has been mulling substantive changes to officer management for at least a decade. In 2002, for example, the DoD Under Secretary for Personnel and Readiness asked "How should military officer force management change to better balance breadth of experience (generalization) with depth of experience (specialization)?" and "Should we slow down assignments (i.e., increase assignment tenure)...?"[25] Additionally, in 2006, the *Quadrennial Defense Review* (QDR) called for the DoD to "foster innovation by encouraging [new] career patterns that develop the unique skills needed to meet new missions..."[26]

As recently as January 2011, the Defense Science Board (DSB) noted that "... the rapid ... timelines for leadership change in the DoD have resulted in a culture that can 'wait out' [strategic] initiatives," and that "DoD incentives are largely compliance-driven rather than results-focused, which leads the Department too often to optimize around process rather than delivering capability...."[27] Much like the GAO, the DSB also called for better personnel information systems, citing recent Army efforts to align officer talents with organizational demand as a positive move in that direction.[28] A month later, Secretary of Defense Gates characterized the "greatest challenges facing the Army" in this way:

> How can the Army break-up the institutional concrete, its bureaucratic rigidity in its assignments and promotion processes? ... Just as the Army has reset and reformed itself when it comes to doctrine, equipment, and training, it must ... attack the institutional and bureaucratic constipation of Big Army....[29]

For its part, the Army knows it must respond to these challenges and has been contemplating how to do so for years. Take, for example, the 2001 *Army Training and Leader Development* (ATLD) study, a comprehensive examination of the ways in which it develops and employs leaders. Calling for a more "self-aware and adaptive" officer corps, among other challenges, the study identified universal, linear career paths as an obstacle to these goals:

> Assignment requirements, *instead of individual leader development needs*, drive officer personnel management. DA Pam 600–3, Commissioned Officer Development and Career Management, *focuses on career gates rather than the quality of developmental experiences.... The Army assignments system is driven by requirements to fill spaces....* Officers and field commanders have little say in the current process.[30]

While this viewpoint has remained relatively consistent, thoughts on how to meet the challenge have varied across time. For example, the Army's 2006 *Review of Education, Training and Assignments for Leaders* (RETAL Study), published near the nadir of American fortunes in Iraq, found that officers were generally equal to the demands of warfighting but were less adept in "nonkinetic competencies."[31] It concluded that to prevail in the future, every Army officer must become a "pentathlete," a "multi-skilled warrior leader . . . strategic thinker/decisionmaker . . . business manager/enterprise leader . . . team builder/leader developer . . . and diplomat."[32] To facilitate this, the report recommended creating "Leader Development Assignment Panels" (LDAP) to identify and provide "the best operational career field officers with . . . development opportunities emphasizing mental agility, enterprise management, or cross-cultural savvy."[33]

In other words, the RETAL Study suggested that sprinkling more unconventional, nonoperational assignments upon the traditional career population of fast-tracking operations types would help them broaden into pentathletes—they could do it all. Whether

LDAP selectees would welcome such nonoperational assignments (which traditionally entail career risk) wasn't addressed, nor was the future career prospects of non-selectees, many of whom might possess the very nonoperational talents needed for effective institutional management.

Over time, the discussion of adaptability evolved, with diminished emphasis upon "every officer a pentathlete." By 2009, the *Army Leader Development Strategy* was calling instead for "a mix of generalists and specialists that *collectively* provide diverse talents to meet all of the Army's requirements. . ."[34] This was amplified in the Army's *Capstone Concept*, published later that same year. It sought a future officer corps that:

> . . . exhibit[s] critical thinking, comfort with ambiguity and decentralization, a willingness to accept prudent risk, *and an ability to make rapid adjustments*. . . . The Army must also . . . expand efforts to develop leaders who have *expertise in relevant disciplines* through broadening experiences and . . . *high quality graduate education*. . . .[35]

By 2010, this ongoing introspection seemingly reached a culminating point, as the Army's Human Capital Enterprise co-chairs (the Assistant Secretary of the Army for Manpower and Reserve Affairs and the Commanding General, U.S. Army Training and Doctrine Command) hosted a multiday conference focused upon officer **talent management**—a paradigm recognizing that every person possesses a unique distribution of skills, knowledge, and behavior that allows that person to perform optimally in one or more areas, provided his or her talents are identified, cultivated, and liberated.[36]

As a result, today's Army leaders recognize the need for more than adaptable senior officers. They also desire a flexible talent management system that translates the unique capabilities of each senior officer into true institutional adaptability. Witness the Secretary of the Army's clarion call for a complete redesign of the Army's people management policies and processes:

> My passion for transforming the Generating Force [Institutional Army] . . . will shape my tenure as Secretary. . . . Meeting these challenges requires truly transforming how we manage our people . . . *achieving institutional adaptability through a . . . system that rapidly responds to organizational requirements for talent.*[37]

Clearly, a chorus of government, defense, and Army voices is seeking increased institutional adaptability via improved senior officer development and employment, an evolution from one-size-fits-all, time-based personnel management to individually tailored, productivity-focused talent management. While there is much to do in that regard, a synthesis of their critical concerns yields five key change imperatives:

1. Differentiate people—seek and employ a diverse range of talents.
2. Develop relevant and specialized expertise via individual career paths.
3. Invest in higher and specialized education.
4. Improve succession planning.
5. Provide sufficient assignment tenure.

We think these are spot on, and strong evidence from studies of organizational and human capital management supports their efficacy. But they cannot work if merely bolted on to current officer management practices, which in many respects have gone unchanged for almost 65 years. Senior officer management must be firmly rooted within a comprehensive Army-wide evolution towards all-ranks officer talent management, one which provides both the structural and career flexibility needed to respond to whatever unanticipated crises the future may bring.

In this book, we will first articulate a foundational framework for that comprehensive evolution. We will examine the five change imperatives, identify the undesirable consequences of current practices, and suggest evolutionary alternatives grounded in sound theory and tailored to the Army profession. These alternatives, if thoughtfully executed, will create a talent management system that accounts for officer continuation (retention) behavior, restores discretion to promotions, builds a versatile and diverse talent bench, and thus strengthens the Army profession. We will make our suggestions from a spirit of service, not criticism, but to be clear—we think much of the current officer management system should be revised. Past practices should serve as handrails, not handcuffs. The time for contemplation is over. With a significant drawdown underway, it is time for action.

ENDNOTES - CHAPTER 2

1. Peter Drucker was one of the most influential thinkers on the subject of management theory and practice. His writings predicted many of the major developments of the late 20th century, including privatization and decentralization; the decisive importance of marketing; and the emergence of the information society and its necessity of lifelong learning. In fact, Drucker coined the term "knowledge worker" in 1959.

2. As was the case in Jack Welch's early days at General Electric. When Welch became CEO, GE was the 10th largest American company by annual earnings and comfortably profitable.

But Welch recognized that the business landscape was changing, particularly as Japanese companies began to eat into GE's market share across several product sectors. The challenge presented GE with an opportunity to reinvent itself, and it emerged as the most profitable American company by the year 2000.

3. Thomas Friedman and Michael Mandelbaum, *That Used to Be Us*, New York: Farrar, Straus, and Giroux, 2011, p. 92.

4. Harry Elsinga, former GE Manager of Executive Development, says that "Expertise . . . builds confidence. If you know a particular area really well, that brings confidence, which allows for creative risk taking." See Leslie Knudson's "Generating Leaders GE Style," *HR Management Online*, p. 1.

5. According to the 2011 Center for Army Leadership Annual Survey of Army Leadership, interpersonal tact is consistently rated as needing the most improvement across all leader levels.

6. Time span of discretion is a concept developed by Elliott Jacques, an organizational psychologist (and also father of the term "mid-life crisis"). Jacques argued that the longer an employee's time span of discretion, the higher his or her compensation should be, as it means the person's work is more strategic and complex, therefore having higher value-producing likelihood.

7. The Peter Principle was formulated by Dr. Laurence J. Peter and Raymond Hull in their eponymous 1969 book.

8. Leadership scholar Ronald Heifetz of Harvard's Kennedy Center characterizes strategic leadership in its purest form as "mobilizing people in response to an adaptive challenge." In other words, strategic leadership = leading change. See Heifetz, *Leadership Without Easy Answers*, Cambridge, MA: Harvard University Press, 1994.

9. According to the Government Accountability Office (GAO), successful change management in large public sector organizations often takes from 5 to 7 years. See *Results-Oriented Cultures: Implementation Steps to Assist Mergers and Organizational Transformations*, GAO-03-669, Washington, DC: GAO, July 2003, p. 9.

10. Joseph E. Stiglitz and Linda J. Bilmes, "The True Cost of the Iraq War: $3 Trillion and Beyond," *The Washington Post*, September 5, 2010, available from *www.washingtonpost.com/wp-dyn/content/article/2010/09/03/AR2010090302200.html*.

11. Don Peck, "Can the Middle Class Be Saved?" *The Atlantic*, September 2011, pp. 60-78.

12. Stiglitz and Bilmes.

13. *Ibid*.

14. *Ibid*.

15. There will be no peace dividend after the Iraq and Afghan wars, which will remain very costly long after the last American Soldier has returned home. More than 800,000 veterans of both wars receive government medical care. The eventual cost of caring for Afghan vets alone will likely eclipse $1 trillion, while Tricare costs will soon represent 10 percent of all defense spending. The VA's annual budget alone is approaching $140 billion (up from $50 billion in 2001). These costs will substantially reduce American military capabilities in the years ahead. See Joseph E. Stiglitz and Linda J. Bilmes, available from *threetrilliondollarwar.org*.

16. For more information on this subject, see *Future Work Skills, 2020*, Phoenix, AZ: Institute for the Future, University of Phoenix Research Institute, 2012.

17. *Army 2025: Title X Challenges*, Washington, DC: Army Directed Studies Office, Western Hemisphere Branch, April 2012, p. 6. Italics are ours.

18. Larrabee, p. 103.

19. Jay Rockefeller and Michael Chertoff, "A New Line of Defense in Cybersecurity," *Washington Post*, November 18, 2011, p. 19.

20. Richard Clarke, "China's Cyberassault on America," *The Wall Street Journal*, June 15, 2011, available from *online.wsj.com/article/SB10001424052702304259304576373391101828876.html?mod=googlenews_wsj*.

21. Lieutenant General Rhett Hernandez, Commanding General, U.S. Army Cyber Command, interview with authors, West Point, NY, October 28, 2011.

22. Harry J. Thie, Margaret C. Harrell, Clifford M. Graf II, and Jerry M. Sollinger, *General and Flag Officers: Consequences of Increased Tenure*, Santa Monica, CA: Rand Corporation, 2001, pp. xi-xiv.

23. Exposure Draft, *A Model of Strategic Human Capital Management*, GAO-02-373SP, Washington, DC: GAO, March, 2002, pp. 4-8.

24. Committee on Armed Services (Subcommittee on Oversight and Investigations), *Another Crossroads? Professional Military Education Two Decades after the Goldwater Nichols Act and the Skelton Panel*, Washington, DC: U.S. House of Representatives, April 2010, p. xii.

25. Office of the Under Secretary of Defense (Personnel and Readiness), *Military Personnel Human Resources Strategic Plan*, Washington, DC: DoD, 2002, Appendix C.

26. *Quadrennial Defense Review Report*, Washington, DC: DoD, February 6, 2006, p. 80.

27. Defense Science Board, *Enhancing Adaptability of U.S. Military Forces, Part A. Main Report*, Washington, DC: Office of the Under Secretary of Defense for Acquisition, Technology and Logistics, January, 2011, p. 9.

28. *Ibid.* p. 124.

29. Secretary of Defense Robert Gates, Speech at West Point, NY, February 25, 2011, available from *www.defense.gov/Speeches/Speech.aspx?SpeechID=1539*. His point is not unlike one made by Harvard leadership scholar Ronald Heifetz, who argues that leadership at the institutional or corporate level first requires correct identification of very complex problems rather than an unduly rapid exercise of "decisive" leadership. See Heifetz, *Leadership Without Easy Answers*, Cambridge, MA: Harvard University Press, 1994.

30. *Army Training and Leader Development Panel Officer Study Report to the Army*, 2001, p. OS-9. Italics are ours.

31. *Ibid.*, p. 7.

32. *Review of Education, Training and Assignments for Leaders (RETAL), Officer Team Report*, Washington, DC: HQDA, November 2006, pp. 4-5.

33. *Ibid.*, p. 9.

34. *2009 Army Leader Development Strategy*, p. 11. Italics are ours.

35. *The Army Capstone Concept*, Washington, DC: U.S. Army Training and Doctrine Command, 2009, pp. 16-23. Italics are ours.

36. This was the 47th Annual Army Senior Conference, co-chaired by the Honorable Thomas Lamont, Assistant Secretary of the Army/Manpower and Reserve Affairs, and General Martin Dempsey, CG, TRADOC at West Point, NY, June 7-9, 2010.

37. Secretary of the Army Memorandum for the Assistant Secretary of the Army for Manpower and Reserve Affairs, June 20, 2011. Italics are ours.

CHAPTER 3

CREATE A FLEXIBLE TALENT MANAGEMENT FRAMEWORK

> ... How do we ensure that we're developing our ... leaders, managing their talents ... for the betterment of both themselves and the institution?[1]
>
> General Martin Dempsey

As we have already described, senior officer management must be firmly rooted within a comprehensive, all-ranks officer talent management framework, one which provides both the structural and career flexibility needed to respond to whatever unanticipated crises the future holds. As Figure 3-1 illustrates, this is because the Army is characterized by very limited lateral entry.[2] Unlike corporate entities, it cannot poach mid-career or senior talent from other firms. This makes junior officers the feedstock for senior officers and amplifies the importance of getting accessions right. Beyond this, the junior and mid-career phases must develop, retain, employ, and continuously evaluate that feedstock to create the depth and breadth of talent needed on the Army's senior officer bench. Such breadth and depth mitigates uncertainty and reduces future risks.

Certainly the Army has always accessed, developed, retained, and employed officers, but as interchangeable parts rather than as unique individuals. What makes our model different, however, is a talent concept firmly grounded in sound human capital theory. By now, readers unfamiliar with our previous work may be asking "What exactly **is** talent?" "Who has it?" and "Doesn't the Army already manage it?"[3]

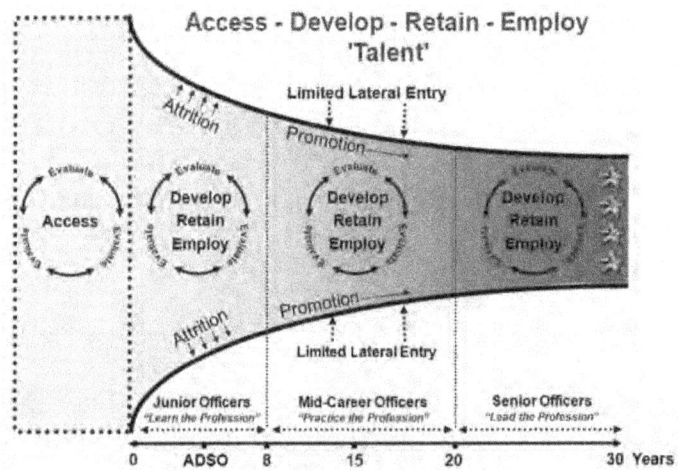

Figure 3-1. The Army Officer Human Capital Model.

Talent is not some "top 10 percent" of workers. It is the unique intersection of skills, knowledge, and behaviors in each of us. Everyone has talents that can be extended and liberated, provided those talents are recognized and cultivated. Doing so creates optimal levels of performance in a much larger segment of an organization's workforce. Right now, however, the Army does not manage officer talent because it lacks effective mechanisms for revealing and capturing those talents (or the demand for them).

Talent embodies a number of dimensions, all combining to create the productive capacities of each person. It represents far more than the training, education, and experiences provided by the Army. The fullness of people's life experiences, to include investments they have made in themselves, personal and familial relationships (networks), ethnographic and demographic background, preferences, hobbies, travel, personality, learning style, education, and a myriad number of other factors better suit them to some development or employment opportunities than others. As we explained in an earlier publication:

> The Army knows plenty about each officer—their home of record, gender, race, marital status, colleges attended, blood type and religion. It tracks their health and fitness levels, months deployed, and awards or decorations. It knows many other things as well – the number and type of training courses completed, positions held, dates of promotion, and security clearance levels. All of this information, and more, is found in each officer's "record brief" (ORB). Unfortunately, this is simple accounting data. To employ officer talent, however, the Army needs *decision support* data, information that reveals what makes each officer *tick*. What do they value? What opportunities do they desire? What incentives will they respond to? What do they know that the Army has not taught them? Where have they been that the Army has not sent them? What do they enjoy? How do they see the future? How do they learn? *In other words, what are their talents?*[4]

Without such accurate, granular data, the Army has little choice but to manage officers via policies that treat them as interchangeable parts, shunting them along standardized career paths in an effort to identify and select a relative handful of operationally adept general officers.

Therein lies a significant part of the challenge we are addressing here—the Army's current one-size-fits-all personnel management approach is unsuited to producing the depth and breadth of senior officer talents that are increasingly in demand. Consider Figure 3-2. Dark grey represents officers with expertise required in the highly specialized and increasingly complex business side of the institutional Army: budgets, personnel management, weapons system procurement and development, information technology, recruiting, marketing, civil-military relations, education, public affairs, etc. Light grey represents officers with the land combat expertise needed to succeed from the platoon to the theater/national level.

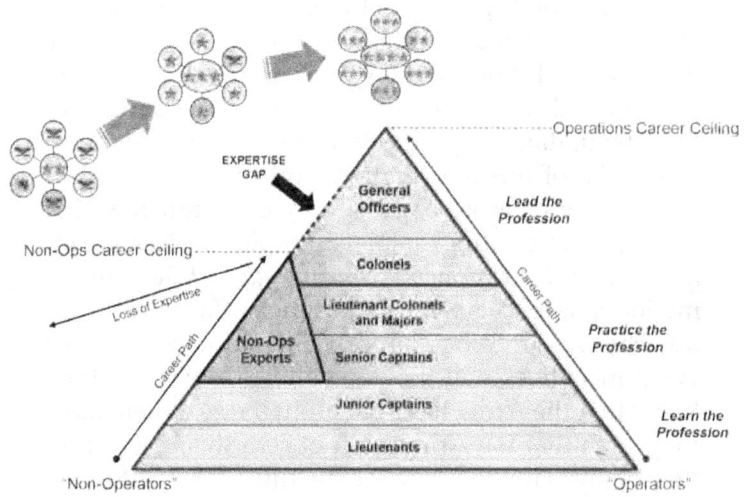

Figure 3-2. Current Paths to Senior Army Leadership.

Due to both policy and tradition, those reaching the top of the Army are usually "maneuver, fires, and effects" officers (particularly "maneuver" and "fires") whose careers heavily transit operational assignments. As the 2001 Army Training and Leader Development (ATLD) panel and others have pointed out, many officers follow the traditional, command-centric career path not because it better prepares them for institutional leadership but because it gives them a better chance of getting there. On their way up, these officers experience exponential increases in their spans of control and business responsibilities, usually with little specialized education to prepare them for the new world of "enterprise" management. Simultaneously, they endure increasingly rapid job rotation, foregoing the assignment tenure so critical to successful change management and strategic leadership. They are extremely talented, they have played by the rules, and some of them **are** expert in nonoperational matters. But as we pointed out in Chapter 2, many are flirting with the "Peter principle" because the Army has not prepared them for nonoperational work.

Figure 3-3 shows that 80 percent of colonel-and-above billets are nonoperational in nature. As Figure 3-4 indicates, however, an outsized number of these billets are occupied by "maneuver/fires" officers who, through no fault of their own, may lack the expertise needed to succeed in institutional/enterprise leadership and management positions.[5] Conversely, non-maneuver/fires officers are far less likely to enter the general officer cohort, bumping up against a lower career ceiling that gives them little option but to take their career field expertise outside the Army.

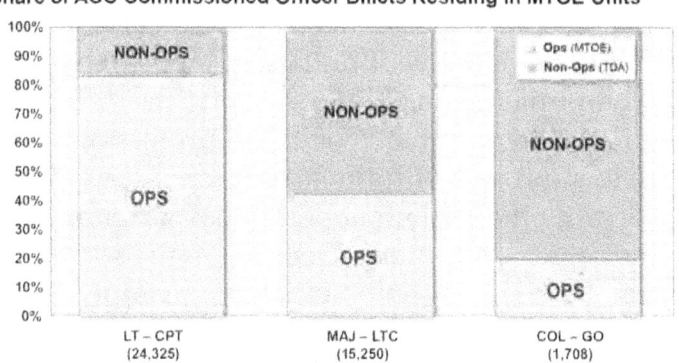

Source: US Army Office of Economic and Manpower Analysis. Statistics were derived from authors' calculations based upon Active Army Authorization Data dated September 30, 2011. All calculations include Army Competitive Category officers plus Medical Service.

Figure 3-3. Operational Billets Decline with Increasing Rank.

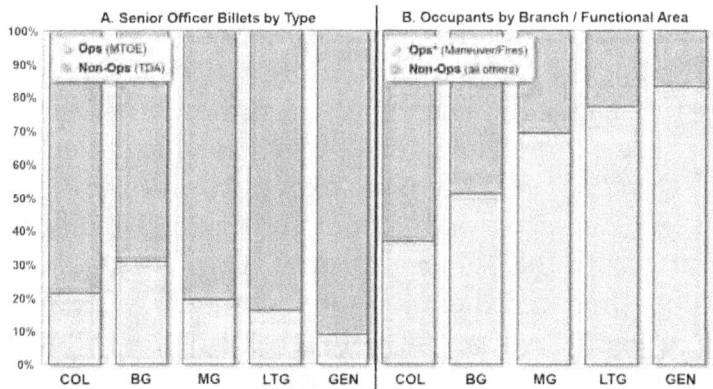

Source U S Army Office of Economic and Manpower Analysis
*Note For General Officers, their last control branch or functional area prior to becoming a general is used

Figure 3-4. Senior Officer Billets versus Occupants, 2011.

In other words, the Army recognizes the need to cultivate land combat and nonoperational experts in its officer corps. It competitively selects certain officers for development as strategists, economists, human resource and financial managers, political scientists, etc. It invests millions of dollars in their higher education. And then, almost inexplicably, the Army eats its young, denying many of these professionals the chance to improve institutional efficacy and adaptability as senior officers in nonoperational assignments.

This begs the question, "Does the Army sometimes advance the wrong senior officers or simply fail to provide them with the right development?" The answer is yes on both counts. As the range of national security challenges becomes increasingly asymmetric and nonkinetic, winnowing talent by herding it down narrow career paths denies the Army the bench strength needed to meet them. Success in warfighting, nation building, disaster relief, and myriad other contingencies requires an organizational breadth **and** depth of talent that can be achieved only by creating more pathways to senior officer leadership.

As illustrated in Figure 3-5, such an approach allows business and management excellence to complement (not replace) the operational acumen needed at the top of a land combat profession. It closes expertise gaps at the institutional level, creating a versatile distribution of senior officers that can respond more rapidly to unforeseen challenges. It builds both depth and breadth of talent: operations/land combat experts (C), nonoperational experts (A), and some officers possessing both the operational **and** institutional expertise demanded at the very top of the profession (B). Essentially, this approach helps the Army "catch up" with the talent management practices used by innovative American companies for over 2 decades. It is an important thing to do, as domestic firms are fierce competitors for many of the talents so critical to the Army's success.

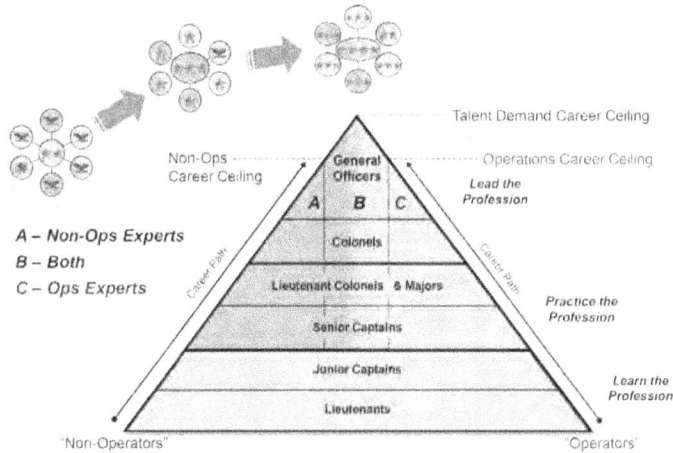

Figure 3-5. Expanded Pathways to Senior Army Leadership.

Implementing such a system requires dismantling several legacy practices, however. Figure 3-6 maps current active duty officer requirements (the descending black line) across the officer service continuum. As we can see, the officer talent pipeline begins with land combat apprentices who over time become fully fledged practitioners of the Army profession. Those practitioners in turn become the feedstock for the profession's senior leaders who command, serve as institutional executives, or advise military and civil authorities. In fact, all senior officer duties embody one or more of these roles.

It is intuitive that junior officers spend the bulk of their early careers in operational assignments, where fairly uniform experiences provide the normative foundation for land combat professionals. As they move into mid-career, however, these officers encounter a fundamental obstacle to identifying and liberating their talents—management and promotion by year group. This is the rigid backbone of the Army's up-or-out, command-centric management system, and a host of negative consequences cascade from it.

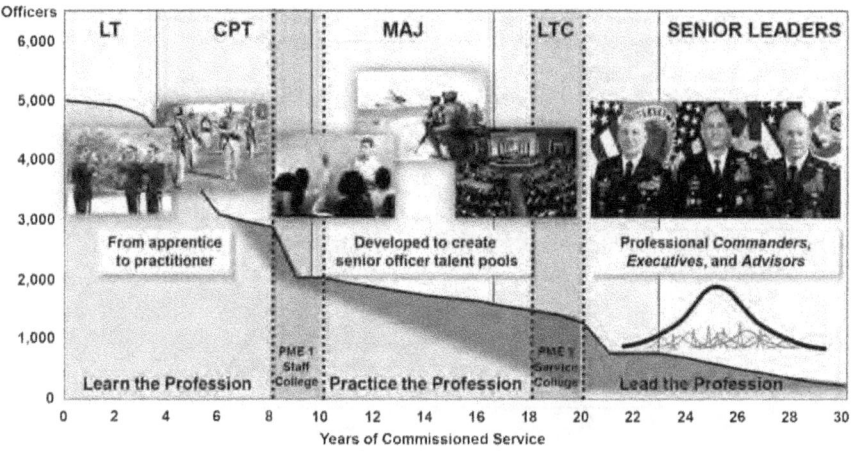

Figure 3-6. Officer Service Continuum.

First and foremost, it stifles the differentiation of people, evaluating all officers against a unitary, command-centric ideal, thus discouraging many from seeking the "nontraditional" assignments that would better prepare them for institutional leadership. Year-group management also denies officers job opportunities they would be ideally suited to because they are too junior in rank, lack a requisite "key/developmental assignment," or are in some way ineligible due to other standardized career path obstacles. This creates a management culture focused upon who is available for the job (by rank/time in service) rather than who is best for it (by talent).

This flies in the face of previously successful practices demonstrated by the Army in the modern era. Had this management system been in place during World War II, for example, not only would General Dwight Eisenhower have failed to rise to command of all Allied Forces in Europe, but General Creighton Abrams might have languished as a regimental adjutant rather than lead an armored combat command, and General Curtis LeMay would have perhaps remained a squadron commander in Europe rather than lead the successful Pacific air campaign. In their day, when the talent for a particular job was present, the assignment was made and the commensurate rank was then provided.

In sum, year-group management, with its focus on administrative ease and supposed fairness, retards the identification and development of talent across the board. As Figure 3-7 illustrates, it also creates officer inventory excesses and shortages. That is why we recommend eliminating year-group management at the 8th year of commissioned service. This would allow the Army to differentiate officers by talent rather than time-in-grade, assigning them where their abilities dictate and promoting them accordingly. It would also end lock-step career paths, essentially giving mid-career officers a decade to practice their profession and prepare for senior leadership, unencumbered by assignments or developmental opportunities that may not match their particular talents or needs.

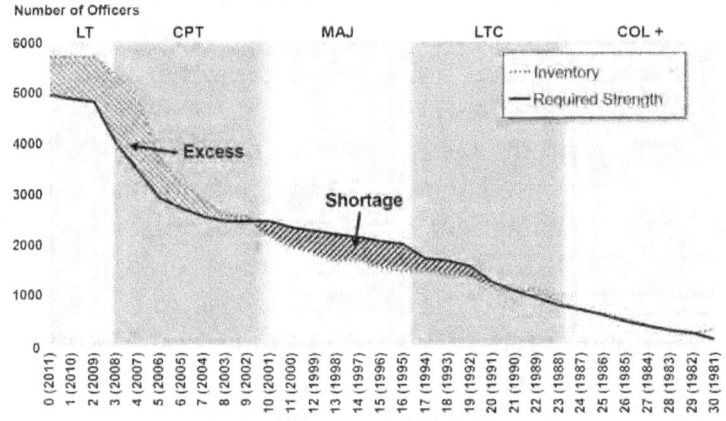

Years of Service (Year Group) as of September 2011
Source US Army Office of Economic and Manpower Analysis

Figure 3-7. Current Officer Inventory Excesses and Shortages.

To do this, however, a companion innovation is required—the implementation of comprehensive talent assessments as officers approach their 8th and 20th years of service (YOS). We will place this within a larger evaluative context in the next chapter, but briefly, here is the rationale (see Figure 3-6).

- **Officers approaching 8 YOS** are completing their "apprenticeship" (as well as their 8-year military service obligation). It is the right time to assess their suitability for full entry into the profession and to manage them by talent rather than year group. This is now possible because they have amassed a significant performance history, one that allows the Army to divine their unique talents (and talent gaps). The 8-year mark also requires a retention incentive. By selecting officers for continued service/promotion to major by this year (with a later pin on point), the Army gains a powerful retention tool, ensuring it has a sufficiently deep bench of mid-career officers to allow for genuine talent management. This is also a significant culling point—officers who are a poor talent match for the Army are encouraged to seek a different career or separated from service as the situation warrants. Finally, functional designation takes place here, recognizing the strengths and desires of each officer and identifying the appropriate talent domain in which he or she can excel.

- **Officers approaching 20 YOS** are completing the "practitioner" phase of the profession and are poised to lead it as senior officers. Fully vested in their pension plans, some are contemplating retirement and life outside of the Army. It is the right time to assess their suitability for "executive" leadership with this proviso—"if we retain you, you are immediately eligible for **any** senior officer position in the Army (O-6 and above) should you be the best talent match." By selecting officers for continued service by this point, the Army forestalls the 20th year retirement impulse of many mid-career officers, creating a deeper bench of senior officer talent critical to institutional leadership and management.

These initiatives will provide an overarching officer talent management framework, one that creates a stable balance between officer requirements and inventory. That balance will restore discretion to promotion opportunity and timing, allowing the Army to screen, vet, and cull officer talent. To do this effectively, however, the Army must begin to differentiate its officers at all ranks.

ENDNOTES - CHAPTER 3

1. Comments made at the 47th Annual U.S. Army Senior Conference, West Point, NY, June 6-8, 2010.

2. Could this change a bit? Yes. The Army could probably open the lateral entry aperture somewhat, particularly in emerging technology areas. For example, Frank Capra was arguably the best War Information Officer of World War II. A Hollywood filmmaker-turned-Signal Corps major, his *Why We Fight* movies explained the U.S. entry into the war in powerful and understandable terms. George Marshall commissioned Capra because such high-quality film production was beyond the Army's abilities in 1941. That said, expanded lateral entry is unlikely to affect the land combat domain. In other words, while the Army may succeed in poaching mid-career technical experts from several fields, its warfighting imperative ensures that much of the officer corps will remain a closed labor market.

3. For a fuller examination of these issues, see the Officer Corps Strategy Monograph Series, Carlisle, PA: Strategic Studies Institute, U.S. Army War College.

4. Casey Wardynski, David S. Lyle, and Michael J. Colarusso, *Towards a U.S. Army Officer Corps Strategy for Success: Employing Talent*, Carlisle, PA: Strategic Studies Institute, U.S. Army War College, May 2010, p. 9.

5. Note that in Figures 3-3 and 3-4, we used Modified Table of Organization and Equipment (MTO&E) versus Table of Distribution & Allowance(s) unit assignments to parse officers into operational and non-operational categories. To check our work, we also parsed officer positions by organizational function and echelon. No matter how we sliced it, the results were similar — between 70 and 80 percent of senior officer positions inordinately require enterprise leadership and management acumen rather than land combat expertise.

CHAPTER 4

DIFFERENTIATE PEOPLE

Differentiation breeds meritocracy; sameness breeds mediocrity.[1]

Bill Conaty and Ram Charan,
The Talent Masters

"Late bloomer" describes those who unexpectedly hit their stride and begin performing in standout fashion after years of unremarkable work. Sometimes it is the result of individual experimentation, as a person discovers and refines his or her talents. Consider Cézanne, who became famous not for his earliest paintings, but for the impressionist art he produced in his 60s[2] or "Colonel" Harlan Sanders, the failed insurance salesman who began the Kentucky Fried Chicken (KFC) Corporation with a portion of his first Social Security check.[3] Other times, it is due to chance or crisis (think Ulysses Grant — uninspired harness shop clerk, great military strategist). Occasionally, it is due to the support and belief of others — inventor Franklin Leonard Pope taking in a down-and-out young telegraph operator named Thomas Edison, for example.

The key point is that all people are unique. Whether late bloomer or child prodigy, people have it within themselves to perform better. Figuring out what they do well and which development will maximize their performance is called **differentiation**, the first step to unlocking the latent productive capacities of any workforce.

In a knowledge economy, where work is more interconnected, technical, specialized, and complex, differentiation is increasingly critical, and the best employers recognize this. General Electric, for example, which for years groomed jack-of-all-trades types for its top jobs, has in the last decade adjusted its executive development philosophy to cultivate more deep industry experts instead. Differentiating talent by expertise has also increased assignment tenure, allowing GE to rotate people less frequently from job to job.[4]

To effectively differentiate people, an organization must clearly articulate the diverse range of talents needed in its workforce. It must also create a management culture that appreciates and employs those talents. An examination of the Army's current practices reveals that, for the most part, it does neither.

CURRENT PRACTICES

To be clear, the Army does differentiate its officers. Unfortunately, it is generally as "above center of mass" and "everyone else," a bimodal distribution created in part by measuring all officers against an operational, command-centric ideal. It relies chiefly upon two assessment mechanisms. The first is the one-size-fits-all Officer Evaluation Report (OER), the Army's chief evaluative instrument. The rating inflation and generic information endemic to the current OER makes it a very ineffectual talent differentiation tool. We have previously described it in this way:

> The current Officer Evaluation Report . . . seeks a *particular* talent distribution in every individual, despite the widely differing distributions of skills, knowledge and behaviors required to perform optimally as an infantry platoon leader versus a signal company com-

mander versus an acquisitions colonel. Evaluating all officers against the same generic criteria hides talent from the Army and makes it far less effective than it could be. In short, the current Officer Evaluation Report, the Army's centerpiece screening, vetting, and culling tool, is an increasingly toothless instrument. . . .[5]

The second assessment mechanism consists of competitive selection boards for promotion, command, or opportunities such as senior service college. In reaching their decisions, board members unfortunately rely most heavily upon ineffectual OERs, augmented by simple "accounting" data for each officer (Army and civil schools attended, overseas/combat deployments, additional skill identifiers, health and deployability, official photo, awards, disciplinary or adverse actions, etc.). A Memorandum of Instruction (board guidance) is also issued to each board (i.e., value this, not that).[6]

And that's it. There is no interview to establish an officer's career goals or retention risk, no certification exams, no inventory of professional capabilities, no psychometric assessments of learning style or personality, etc. In short, nothing is done to gain an intimate knowledge of each individual before making decisions that could ultimately result in his or her departure from the Army. The board process is entirely a paper one, with perhaps seconds spent evaluating years of work by each officer.

Few world class human resource (HR) systems still manage people this way, and Figure 4-1 helps illustrate why. Imagine it represents an Army command selection board. For ease of discussion, assume a 20 percent selection rate, (10 percent selected to the primary list, 10 percent to the alternate list). Those selected are notified, but the nonselect majority receives no feedback on the outcome. They are instead met with silence from the profession to which they have devoted their lives. For many of them, self-recriminations quickly begin as they ponder the career implications of nonselection. Some may ask a mentor or an assignments officer to explain the unwelcome result. Regardless of how insightful that explanation may be, however, the damage is done—the Army has powerfully signaled that it is not interested in the career of nonselectees, even though it may desire several more years of service from each.

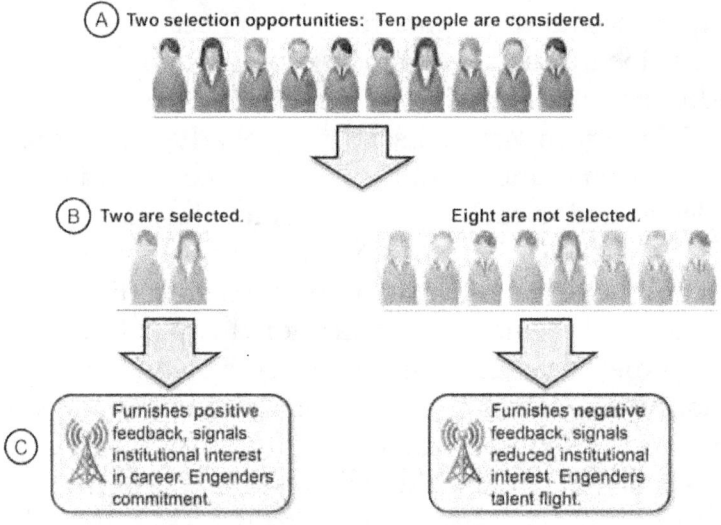

Figure 4-1. Competitive Selection Boards are a Missed Differentiation Opportunity.

Perhaps unwittingly, from here forward, the Army's HR management culture tends to treat these officers as "filler," often placing them in jobs that reinforce their noncompetitiveness for promotion, command, or school. They are now less relevant than those anointed as institutional heirs via board selection. Once out of that club, it is exceedingly difficult to get back in. In organizational research parlance, this is an example of **cumulative advantage**—those perceived as "high potential" employees are given career-enhancing opportunities at the expense of others, who may never receive such opportunities regardless of their later growth or suitability. The earlier a high potential marker is appended to a career (key job success, awards, below-the-zone promotion, etc.), the more powerful the cumulative advantage.[7]

While this can lower productivity and engender talent flight, there is more bad news. Despite annually assembling thousands of career files and convening multiple selection boards to review them, no attempt is made by the Army to reveal and inventory officer talents—nothing new is learned. In fact, because so little is really known about these officers, they are extremely difficult to differentiate. As a result, final selection decisions sometimes hinge upon one evaluation report or even something as superficial as an official photo, which reveals little talent information. In short, competitive selection boards are a missed opportunity to differentiate officers into the widely varied talent pools needed to make the Army more adaptable, particularly at the senior level.

Without sufficient information to differentiate officer talents, and with an inordinate focus upon operational/command ability, how **does** the Army identify and select those senior officers best suited to leading its "nonkinetic" efforts? For the most part, it does not. It continues instead to rely upon information-starved selection boards, whose members tend to advance officers following the same career paths that they did. As one general recently told us, sometimes the implications of such practices are concerning:

> Whenever I attend a Four Star Conference, I'm struck by the fact that the people sitting around the table, although talented and selfless professionals, are remarkably similar to me in age, developmental experiences and world view. And those coming up behind us look equally similar because we're picking them. . . . I sometimes wonder whether we're all too much alike to provide the Chief with the breadth and depth of counsel he needs to navigate the Army towards the future.[8]

His comments are not unlike those of the Bundeswehr's Major General Baron von Freytag-Loringhoven, who argued that "it is highly desirable, even essential . . . that the more influential members of a general's staff not be too much like the general."[9]

Building talent depth and breadth requires differentiation. This in turn requires a comprehensive evaluation **system**, one that provides the Army with an intimate understanding of each officer. That system would rest upon three legs: redesigned OERs; comprehensive periodic assessments of each officer (Individual Development and Employment Assessments, or IDEAs); and a talent management information system that captures the results and renders them truly useful to officers, commanders, and HR managers alike. Evaluative priorities could then shift away from today's inordinate focus upon "promotion and command" and towards the development, credentialing and optimal employment of each officer. As the Army is already redesigning the OER, we will limit our discussion to the benefits of comprehensive periodic assessments and a talent management information system.

COMPREHENSIVE ASSESSMENTS REQUIRE NEW "IDEAS"

In Chapter 3, we suggested comprehensive assessments of all officers approaching their 8th and 20th years of service. For ease of reference, from here on, we will refer to them as IDEAs. IDEAs should take place not just at those points but at key **career crossroads** throughout an officer's military service. Career crossroads are appropriate times to conduct penetrating talent assessments because that is when leadership and management responsibilities shift into higher bands of complexity. Walter Mahler, originator of the career crossroads concept and an early innovator in the realm of succession planning and executive development, argued that these shifts require corresponding changes in an employee's time horizons (i.e., tenure), talents, work values, and education.[10]

As Figure 4-2 illustrates, today an officer may transit up to eight career crossroads from precommissioning to retirement. Executing penetrating talent assessments at several of these crossroads can foster genuine, all-ranks talent management:

- Crossroad 1 (Admissions/Enrollment). This is where talent management truly begins. Incredibly, recruiting efforts here determine the fundamental talent composition of the senior officer corps 30 years in the future. The Army must therefore carefully recruit cadets and officer candidates to meet near-term and long-run talent and demographic diversity demands. While current assessments of new cadets/officer candidates are somewhat rigorous, comparatively little is known about the talent demands they are actually being recruited to meet.[11]

- Crossroad 2 (Branching/Commissioning). Today, little is done by each commissioning source to align individual talents and undergraduate education against the specific needs of the 16 Army basic branches. (This is unfortunate, as doing so would promote talent and demographic diversity in each branch).[12] After branching and commissioning, officers embark upon a period of self-management as each prepares to lead others, culminating in Basic Officer Leader Course (BOLC) certification.
- Crossroads 3 and 4 (Platoon/Company Leadership). Now company grade "apprentices" in the Army profession, officers arrive at Crossroad 3 (platoon leader) when they are entrusted with the leadership of soldiers for the first time. Crossroad 4 (Company Command) brings the responsibility to lead not just soldiers, but also other officers and senior noncommissioned officers. We do not recommend IDEAs at these crossroads, as they fall within the formative period of an officer's career. In these early years, talent differentiation, while important, is less critical than providing a common framework of land combat training, development, and education. This creates the normative baseline of values, tactical expertise, professional language, and shared sacrifice necessary to bond young officers not just to the profession, but also to their soldiers and each other.

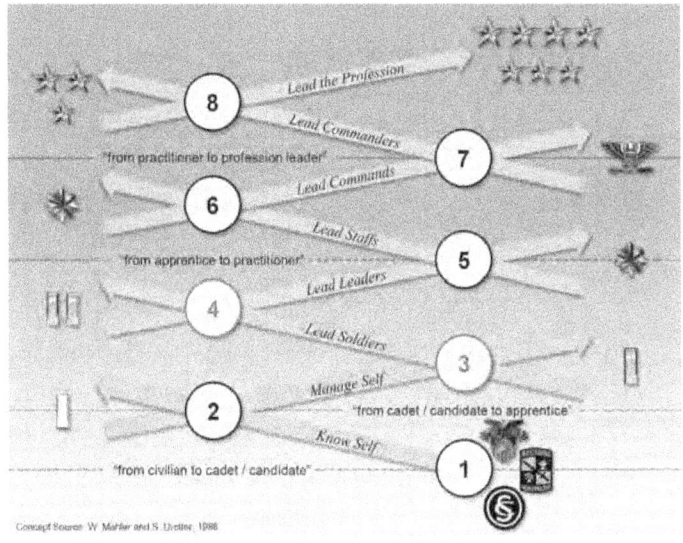

Figure 4-2. Current Officer Career Crossroads.

Up to this point, what we have described is fairly consistent with the Army's current officer development model (although we've pointed out the lack of granular talent management in existing admissions and branching practices). As Figure 4-3 illustrates, however, IDEAs will reveal such a wealth and diversity of talent that from **Crossroad 5** onward, some officers will transit multiple levels of job complexity in one move, whereas others may work for years in assignments of middling complexity, contingent upon their talents and the demand for them. "Up-or-out" will be replaced by "best fit," regardless of time in service:

- Crossroad 5. Officers are nearing completion of their apprenticeship (and 8-year military service obligation). The Army can now assess their suitability for full entry into the profession because they've amassed a significant employment history, one that allows the Army to identify their unique talents (and talent gaps). The 8-year mark also requires a retention incentive. By selecting officers for continued service/promotion to major by this year (with a later pin on point), the Army gains a powerful retention tool, ensuring it has a sufficiently deep bench of mid-career officers to allow for genuine talent management.[13] This is also a significant culling point—officers who are a poor talent match for the Army are encouraged to seek a different career or separated from service as the situation warrants. Lastly, functional designation takes place here, recognizing the strengths and desires of officers and identifying the appropriate talent domain in which they can excel.

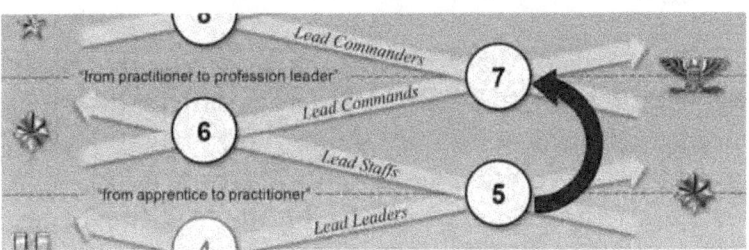

Figure 4-3. IDEAs Reveal Officers
Who Can Transit Multiple Complexity Levels.

- Crossroad 6. Officers are now experienced practitioners of the profession. It is time to reassess their talents against current and emerging demands and to realign them into appropriate/additional talent pools as needed, all with an eye to building future senior leader bench strength. The IDEA conducted here eliminates the need for either battalion command or lieutenant colonel selection boards and can generate the benefits shown in Figure 4-4. In this figure, 10 officers are evaluated via an IDEA panel at Step A. Two are culled from service at Step B because they lack the requisite talents for service in the Army.[14] The remainder are differentiated into the talent pools where each is most likely to excel. As Step C indicates, this furnishes positive feedback to each officer, signaling institutional interest in his or her career longevity and simultaneously increasing trust, the lifeblood of professions.

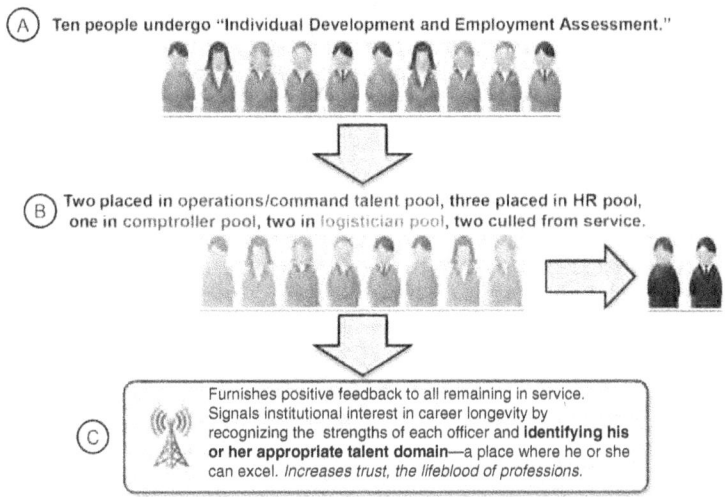

Figure 4-4. IDEAs Replace Competitive Selection Boards.

- Crossroad 7. As officers approach their 20th year of commissioned service, they are completing the "practitioner" phase of the profession and are poised to lead it as senior officers. Fully vested in their pension plans, some are contemplating retirement and life outside of the Army. It is the right time to assess their suitability for "executive" leadership with this

proviso—"if we retain you, you are immediately eligible for **any** senior officer position in the Army should you be the best talent match." By selecting officers for continued service by this point, the Army forestalls the retirement impulse of many mid-career officers, creating a deeper bench of senior officer talent critical to institutional leadership and management.
- Crossroad 8. Senior officers reaching this career crossroad are poised to move to the highest levels of Army leadership. Consistent with the talent information obtained during previous IDEAs, they are formally identified for the truly "key" jobs at the three and four-star levels. Importantly, selection for these jobs is not narrowly limited to current generals—any senior officer is eligible if he or she is the best talent match. This concept will be discussed in greater detail in Chapter 7.

As Figure 4-5 illustrates, integrating career crossroads with the Officer Human Capital Model introduced in Chapter 3 highlights specific points at which the Army can implement innovative officer talent management policies.

IDEA CONCEPT

The prerequisites needed to execute IDEAs are discussed in Chapter 9, but for now, we will focus upon the general concept. Again, the purpose of an IDEA is to gain intimate knowledge of each officer so that his or her unique talents may be developed and employed by the Army, to the mutual benefit of the individual and the institution. What do we mean by intimate knowledge?

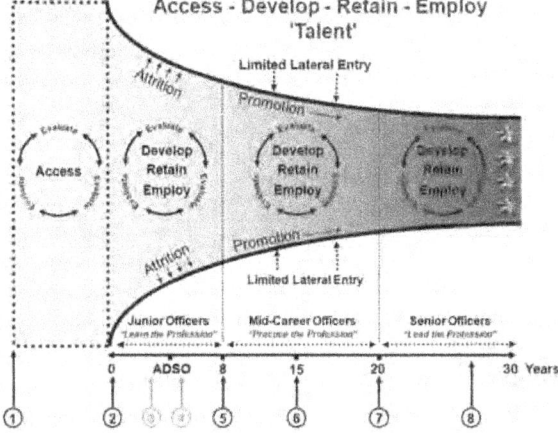

① Admit/Enroll Ensure recruitment into each accessions source supports future demographic and talent diversity in the officer corps

② Branch/Commission Align officer education and talent potential with branch talent demands to foster talent and demographic diversity in each branch

⑤ Retain and Career Field Designate those officers demonstrating the appropriate talent potential for more complex jobs Cease management by year group

⑥ Mid-Career Azimuth Check Review the performance and potential of mid-career officers and adjust their individual career plans accordingly

⑦ Retain beyond 20 years of service (YOS) those officers whose talents suit them to meet the Army's diverse senior officer talent demands

⑧ Promote to Senior Leader anyone in the Senior Officer talent pool Make talent-driven rather than seniority-driven selections

Figure 4-5. Officer Career Crossroads Provide Specific Policy Points.

As Figure 4-6 indicates, an IDEA panel reviews four information sectors: **self-awareness, work evaluation, accounting information**, and a personal **interview**. Each sector relies heavily upon the officer being assessed, as well as upon input from the **mentor**, the **supervisor**, the **administrator**, and the **career counselor**, who consolidates the information and presents it to the IDEA panel.

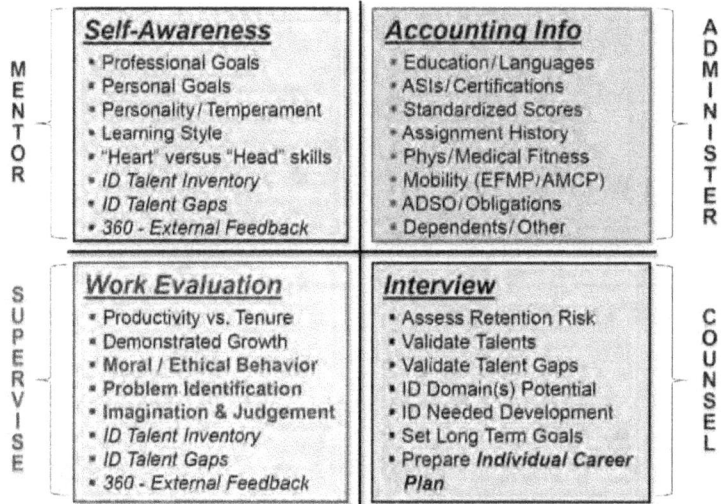

Figure 4-6. IDEA Sectors and Roles.

- Self-Awareness (Mentor). It may seem hard to believe, but after years of conforming to a one-size-fits-all career management system, many officers are largely unaware of their personal talents, developmental, and employment needs. Career introspection is not their strong suit because they have always measured themselves by the same yardstick that the Army has: operational/command talent. The high job churn that makes the Army profession such a restless one also inhibits reflection—there is little time for it.

As a result, officers rarely establish long-term professional goals because the institution does it for them via lock-step career paths. Many are loath to deviate from this because they erroneously equate "selfless service" with "go wherever you are told and do whatever we ask." But it is hard to be selfless without first being self-aware, without knowing how and where one can make the biggest contributions to Army success. This, in turn, requires a talent management environment that recognizes and appreciates the uniqueness of each individual.

Within such an environment, by the 7th year of service, each officer will select a "mentor," a relationship formally acknowledged by the Army. The mentor will be a senior officer outside of their protégé's chain of command, yet possessing expertise germane to his or her development. Along with career counselors (more on them shortly), mentors will become critical members of each officer's personal development team. In a trusting environment, they will help officers formulate career goals, encourage them to conduct candid self-inventories, and offer honest yet confidential talent assessments. This is why the officer must select the mentor—he or she must be comfortable with the person.

While the inherent value of mentorship is already recognized within Army culture and doctrine, in practice, mentorship and patronage are often confused. When we say mentor, we do not mean a senior officer who has sufficient institutional influence to shape future assignments and opportunities for a young officer. While those types of relationships will persist in any workforce, in our view, a "mentor" and "patron" have very different roles and motivations. Well-intentioned patrons are senior officers who (like everyone else) are heavily influenced by their own experiences. Because they are confident in their own contributions, for the betterment of the Army they often seek to advance officers resembling themselves. Mentors, on the other hand, help officers to know themselves. Mentors listen. They advise. They provide wisdom, not institutional influence.

In addition to mentorship, the "self-awareness" sector will rely upon information gathered via self-examination. A variety of existing psychometric tests can be harnessed to this effort: personality and learning styles, and risk behavior assessment tools such as the Army's myPrime, RIASEC analyses, etc.[15]

Finally, 360-degree assessments will help officers understand how they are perceived by others. Collectively, these tools will help officers "see" themselves in high definition. This, in turn, will help them formulate career goals and determine where and how they can make their biggest contributions to the Army.

- Work Evaluation (Supervisor). Each officer's current supervisor (rater) will play a critical role in the IDEA process as well. The supervisor is an additional source of talent inventory information. Supervisors observe daily performance, an excellent vantage point from which to assess moral/ethical behavior, judgment, problem identification and solving, etc. The supervisor's appraisal can help validate (or invalidate) the officer's self appraisal. Supervisors will also help the Army assess not just the officer but also the degree of "match" between the officer and the type of work he or she is currently performing. The best supervisors, of course, will develop and advise their officers, serving as role models and rounding out the wise counsel provided by mentors and career counselors (and as a result, many officers will select a previous supervisor as their formal mentor).

- Accounting Information (Administrator). Accounting information is a vital component of the Army's knowledge about each person. This sector is usually well administered by transactional HR cultures such as the Army's, although there's always room for improvement in terms of type, accuracy, and use of existing data. The HR administrative expert who provides this information to the IDEA team will be much like the Army's current HR records technicians, although aided by better technology and subsequently managing more information about each person. This would include standardized test results such as the Test of Adult Basic Education (TABE) and the Defense Language Aptitude Battery (DLAB), as well as graduate record examinations, scholastic aptitude tests (SATs), etc. Information technology is quickly reducing the required number of records technicians, however. Over time, this will allow forward-looking HR departments to realign a greater share of people and dollars towards career counseling, a hallmark of true talent management.
- Interview (Career Counselor). A career counselor's role will be to professionally advise each officer, to maximize his or her performance and potential.[16] The counselor will be the officer's advocate and career planning partner. Over several years, counselors will gain an intimate knowledge of their clients, one rivaling that of close friends and family members. They will truly know their officers: their lives, desires, families, dreams, aspirations, and concerns. They will achieve this familiarity through constant contact, to include phone conversations,

web-based tools, and frequent interviews with each officer. Unlike the mentor, whose role is more advisory in nature, career counselors will prepare formal individual career plans for their officers, and they'll honestly and accurately represent their clients during IDEAs.

Of those participating in each officer's talent assessment, the role of the mentor is important but that of the career counselor is critical.[17] He or she will add a game changing component to the Army's people management repertoire, representing a shift from transactional HR to **transformational** HR. Career counselors will be true "talent masters," part of a new breed of tenured, certified HR professionals. Expert in performance management rather than requirements management, they will receive certifications from professional bodies such as the National Career Development Association, the National Board of Certified Counselors, and others.[18]

Career counselors should possess demonstrated abilities and graduate-level education in the following areas: behavioral economics; career counseling; career development theory; coaching, consultation and performance improvement; diversity; ethical and legal issues; game theory; HR information management; HR research and evaluation; individual and group counseling; individual and group assessment; industrial and organizational psychology; individual developmental program formulation, management, and implementation; master resilience training; and others. These professionals must be continuously educated and trained to maintain and develop the counseling talents needed to complement their years of experience, and they must thoroughly understand the Army that both they and their clients serve. Career counseling is art and science. It cannot be grounded in the legacy experiences of military retirees, for example. While those experiences can provide a useful foundation to a credentialed career counselor, the right education and expertise must be non-negotiable.

The type of counselors described contrast sharply with today's "assignments officers" who, through no fault of their own, rarely possesses HR management expertise or credentials and are focused (as their title suggests) upon assignments, not performance enhancement. Due to high job turnover, assignments officers do not (and cannot) know their clients intimately—in a typical 30-year career, an officer may have as many as 15-20 assignments officers. By comparison, future career counselors will work as members of stable teams with reasonably small client lists (perhaps 150-200 officers), permitting the creation of professional counselor-client relationships that could span a good chunk of an officer's career. As a result, each career counselor will, over time, accrue a clientele spanning lieutenants to senior officers. The experience in developing the latter should prove invaluable to shaping the former (not unlike the sports agent who represents both promising rookies and veteran athletes).

As for an IDEA panel itself, it must be an independent body of experts, professionals in the science of workforce assessment and performance management, standing completely apart from the Army's process-focused HR mechanisms. Best practices in human resource management help explain why this separation is necessary. While we have tailored it to our discussion of the Army, Figure 4-7 maps the four roles of any world class, forward-looking HR system. Each is critical, yet today's Army HR performs them unevenly at best. We'll revisit this topic in some detail in Chapter 9 (Prepare for Change), but when measured against the figure, today's Army HR is strongest in the **Administrative Expert** role (the one increasingly being outsourced to "shared services" HR firms with cloud-based information technology solutions). It also possesses some strength as an **Employee Relations Expert** but is less influential as a **Strategic Partner** or **Change Agent**, roles that cannot and should not be outsourced.

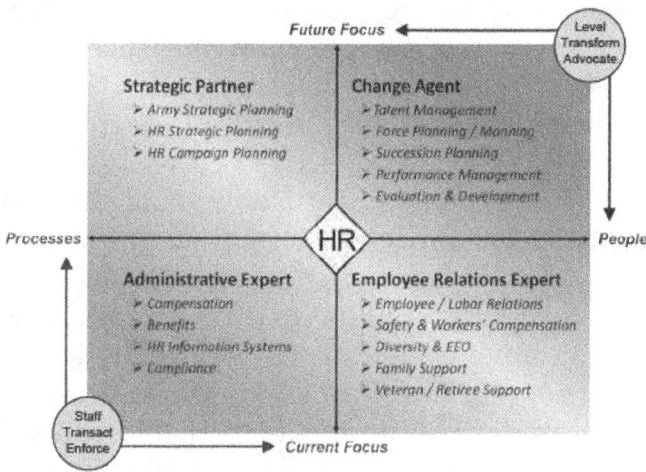

Figure 4-7. Roles and Accountabilities of the Army's HR System.[9]

Army HR is inordinately process driven, its strategic role circumscribed by both policy and practice. This is not because of the Army's HR people, whether on the Army staff or distributed across other organizations. They're all talented and hard-working professionals. It is because of bureaucratic muscle memory built over almost 7 decades. Army HR professionals are trapped in an outmoded design, one that neither prepares them nor permits them to perform these critical HR roles.

In this regard, today's Army HR is not unlike that of other large enterprises still struggling to adapt to the modern era, but its professionals are increasingly aware that many of its inherited personnel practices are unequal to the future. Their biggest challenge is to develop and recommend HR policy changes to the Army leaders who rely upon their expertise. The IDEA process could be one of those changes. Along with other innovations, it can help strengthen Army HR's role as a strategic partner, creating a transformational management system focused more upon people and less upon process. The Army could easily execute a series of nonbinding IDEA pilots, perhaps beginning with a segment of promotable lieutenant colonels or colonels. Small samples of either population would be administratively manageable, and a diverse range of previously unknown yet critical talents would likely be revealed. The results of piloting would validate the concept and provide a roadmap to full implementation.

IDEA Outcomes.

If trust is truly the lifeblood of professions, the transparency and individual focus of IDEAs should dramatically strengthen the Army profession and firmly cement it within a talent management environment. Gone will be the culture of haves and have-nots, with its knee-jerk avoidance of nonoperational assignments. In its place will be a profession with land combat acumen at its center, augmented by a depth and breadth of senior officer talent that allows the institutional Army to adapt rapidly to changes in the governmental, economic, work, and threat environments. The Army will gain an abundance of information about its officers and the ability to build talent pools at every level, each providing the bench strength to meet unforeseen requirements.

IDEA outcomes must be captured and presented in a way that allows leaders to make the best people decisions possible. A critical tool for doing so is the nine-box talent matrix shown at Figure 4-8. In this figure, the numbers do not represent an assessment value but are simply for ease of discussion. For example, an officer whose performance and potential map to Box 1 represents someone who has exceeded every expectation and is ready now to perform perhaps two levels of complexity up. Meanwhile, an officer who maps to Box 6 is low performing but assessed as having high potential.[20]

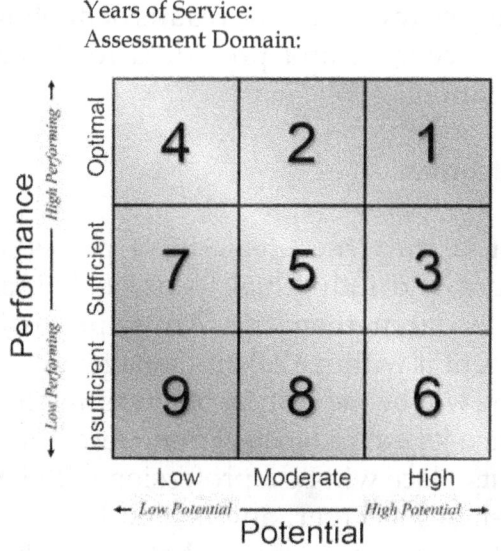

Figure 4-8. The Nine-Box Talent Matrix.

How can this be? In the Army's up-or-out system, an insufficiently **performing** officer could never be deemed high **potential**, as OERs tend to conflate the measurement of each. The answer is that the officer who maps to Box 6 is a talented professional placed in the wrong assignment—a talent mismatch. This type of nuanced assessment is beyond the Army's current capabilities because it has little information on the talents of its people or those demanded by each position. As a result, the performance onus is entirely upon the individual. The institution takes no responsibility for talent mismatches because it cannot detect them.

But IDEAs can reveal the particular talents of each officer, making the nine-box matrix more nuanced still. Note that the top of the matrix has a field titled Assessment Domain. Think of this as an area of needed expertise: operations, logistics, human resource management, etc. It is around these areas that the Army builds its officer talent pools, particularly at the mid-career and senior ranks. Before using the nine-box matrix to assess an officer, it is important to first identify the functional/expertise domain being assessed.

Consider what happens when assessing all people against a single expertise domain. Figure 4-9 is a talent matrix assessing the "operations and command" expertise of five captains at their 8th year of service. As most Army officers "apprentice" in the world of operational assignments during this career phase, there should be sufficient information available to evaluate their operational acumen. Assume that all five are committed professionals, doing their very best each day. In terms of values, general levels of intelligence, fitness, etc., each embodies what the Army demands of commissioned officers.

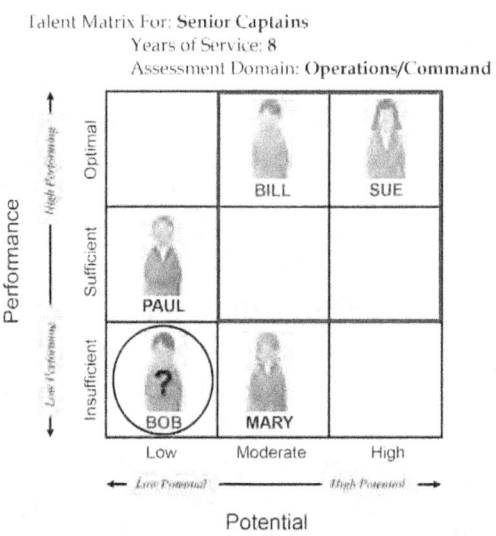

Figure 4-9. Sameness Breeds Mediocrity.

Note that Sue is an apparent superstar—she could command a battalion now if the Army would give her one. Bill is not far behind her, falling easily within the minimum desired performance/potential range. Of course, Paul gets the job done, but he lacks advancement potential—why? Mary is not much better. Sure, she has a bit more potential than Paul, but her performance is truly lackluster. Can she improve?

Then there is Bob, an infantry officer. To put it as politely as possible, he is the kind of fellow you would follow out of sheer curiosity. Low performance, low potential—the guy is an obvious oddball, a misfit. Misfits lack normative baseline talents needed in the Army and should be culled. But before firing Bob, consider this: what if he is not a misfit? What if he's simply a talent **mismatch** for the infantry? What if the IDEA conducted at 8 years of service revealed that Bob, while an ineffectual infantry leader, has an uncanny ability to think in numbers, a logical-mathematical intelligence honed via college and self-study? What if, in addition to a sound physical, professional, and moral-ethical foundation, he has all the makings of an excellent financial manager, something he does in his spare time to support his church or a local charity?[21]

Paul and Mary might benefit from this type of assessment as well. What if the IDEA panel concluded that they were potentially great human resource managers, Paul by temperament and people skills, and Mary by education and experience? The nine-box talent matrix for these officers might look like those at Figure 4-10 instead.

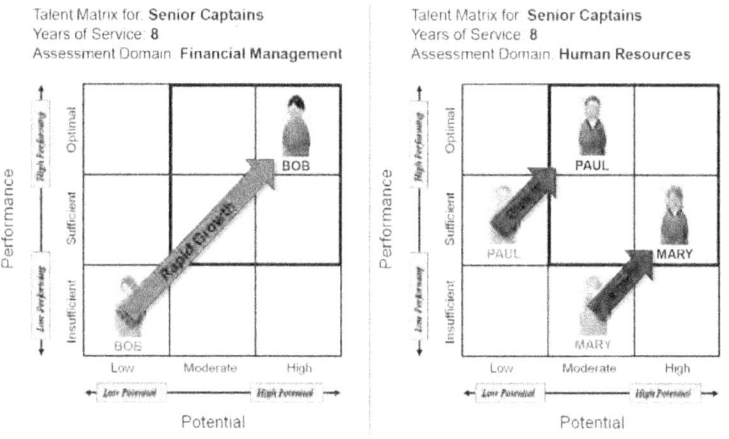

Figure 4-10. Differentiation Breeds Meritocracy.

This type of differentiation is readily achievable via the IDEA process, as deep assessments of performance and potential provide the basis for understanding each officer's capabilities, identifying future roles, and developing them accordingly. This understanding will help the career counselor and officer collaborate in the creation of an individual career plan, which we'll discuss in the next chapter.[22]

A Talent Management Information System.

The assessment process we are describing generates a terrific amount of talent information on the Army's officers, particularly as they approach entry into the senior officer cohort. Volume, however, is counterproductive unless accompanied by accuracy and granularity, not just regarding officer talents but also the demand for those talents across the Army. How can all of this data be captured, organized, and used with telling effect?

The best way to do so is with a secure, web-based talent management system. Its design should proceed from an understanding of how markets work, why they fail, and what can be done to prevent these failures and generate desired outcomes. It should also incorporate behavioral economic theory, which considers how people behave in a market and the incentives needed to engender desired action.[23] With such a capability, the Army could wean itself from reliance upon error-prone requirements forecasts. Instead, it could become a truly adaptable institution, better employing senior officers within their unique talent sets. The Army might then achieve the breadth and depth of capability it needs without requiring every officer to master everything (the pentathlete approach).

This online market place would serve three customer segments: Army officers (the talent supply), Army units (the talent demand), and Army HR (the profession's talent managers or agents). All three have intersecting talent information interests, and each needs an intuitive, rapid, and accurate way to parse that information. In such a marketplace:

- **Officers** (the Supply) would seek employment and developmental opportunities that liberate and extend their talents, allowing them to make an optimal contribution to the Army while pursuing their personal and professional goals. They would derive additional benefits from the system if it provided the introspective tools needed for career planning, as well as others that facilitate knowledge sharing via professional networks. Finally, the system should reveal talent demand signals from the Army and its organizations. This would shape each officer's employment and developmental goals, and the officer would seek to possess talents actually in demand.
- **Units** (the Demand) would seek "ace" job candidates—officers who could dramatically exceed minimal performance because there is a high correlation between their talents and work requirements. They would do this not just by searching the system for talent, but also by populating the system with specific, detailed work requirements for each officer position in their inventory. This would attract the right talent to their organizations. Articulating actual work requirements is critical to making any labor market successful.
- **Army HR** (the Agent) would focus less upon transactions and enforcement and more upon people and performance. The abundance of granular information would create a talent market that "clears" optimally. In other words, as officers and units interact regularly, less intervention would be required by Army HR professionals, who would shift resources and

energies toward talent management and away from requirements management. Taking care of the former is the best way to satisfy the latter.

The information technology solution we are proposing is not original. America's highly regarded people managers (General Electric, Proctor & Gamble, Goodyear, IBM, and others) have been using talent management IT systems for years, liberating their HR staffs from labor intensive, transactional personnel management and freeing up financial and human capital for transformational **talent management**. Those HR departments making best use of this technology are making outsized contributions to their organizations' achievement of strategic goals.

Some readers may be skeptical, questioning the wisdom of benchmarking from the private sector. We are skeptics too. The Army, after all, is a closed labor market, different from the private sector in a myriad number of ways. It cannot poach Maneuver, Fires, and Effects (MFE) officers from Microsoft or John Deere, for example. It must live with the talent it brings in, carefully cultivating that talent to meet its future needs. That is why a talent management IT solution is even **more** critical to the Army—talent shortages cannot be made up elsewhere.

That said, we strongly caution against the implementation of any talent management information system without diligent research and testing of new management techniques. Troweling powerful information technology over an outmoded personnel management edifice may reinforce rather than eliminate legacy practices, making their demolition harder rather than easier. It can also create a false sense that the Army has modernized or "fixed" its HR practices, causing leaders to lose focus on the challenge.

To help guard against such consequences, in 2010, Army leaders asked our office to create a small-scale, proof-of-concept talent management test bed called "Green Pages." Green Pages was not intended as a full-blown defense business system or prototype, and its use will never scale across the officer corps. It is an experimental environment only, lacking the full functionality any future Army talent management solution should possess. Green Pages was constructed, however, with a talent marketplace at its center. That market mechanism is the key.

To date, over 750 active component officers, from captains to lieutenant colonels, have participated in the Green Pages pilot, as have Human Resources Command (HRC) and several branches and career fields. Green Pages uses assignments as its central data entry incentive but not as its overriding purpose. While better talent matches are a significant side benefit, the purpose of a talent management IT solution is to capture accurate, granular information on every officer and every duty position, facilitating the **future** management of each.

Results have been quite promising. Officers in the reassignment window build personal profiles and provide information heavily augmenting their official files, which are also drawn into Green Pages from the Army's Total Army Personnel Database (TAPDB). While officers build their profiles, units with pending vacancies simultaneously build job profiles, elaborating on the talents needed to excel in each officer position. Participating officers review these vacancies and express preferences for them, while units review available officers and express their preferences as well.

Over the span of a few weeks, as officers and units express preferences and communicate directly with one another, a startling thing occurs. Preferences on both sides of the market change, often dramatically. Units reorder their officer selections and officers reorder their unit choices. In fact, half of all participating officers changed their initial assignment preference while exploring the job market.

What is happening is simple. Units are signaling their labor needs, and officers who can meet them are attracted accordingly. Conversely, officers are revealing hidden talents, and units who might not have considered them are suddenly taking notice. During this process, HRC branch representatives facilitate and monitor the market and remain the assignment arbiters—Green Pages is an information marketplace, not a transactional one. Consistent with existing policies and requirements, HRC uses the additional data gathered by Green Pages to optimize assignments.

The Green Pages market mechanism is so effective that even historically "tough fill" posts like Forts Bliss or Polk often have officers eager to be assigned to them. Again, while assignments may be the data entry incentive in Green Pages, the overriding purpose of a talent management system is to capture more talent information for the future. This is critical not just to career planning and succession management, but also to institutional adaptability in time of crisis. For example, of the officers in the pilot (predominately captains), the TAPDB indicated travel spanning 27 percent of the globe. When those officers reported additional travel taking place for higher education, leisure, religious missions, previous civilian employment, prior enlisted service, official temporary duty (TDY), etc., the percentage ballooned to 68 percent.

The cultural fluencies gained via such travel represent potentially millions of dollars in human capital investment, talents the Army did not have to pay for but can readily leverage. In an austere and dynamic threat environment, such information can make the difference between mission success and failure. It can shape drawdown decisions as well. If Green Pages reveals officers with Persian Farsi or Chinese Mandarin language proficiency, and, if those are considered high demand talents, the Army could retain those officers as a hedge against future risks.

The Green Pages pilot makes clear that talent management information systems can reveal the **actual** state of a labor force, the critical asset in any organization. While we have described the immediate benefits of the pilot, they will likely deepen with the acquisition and fielding of a fully featured talent management Defense Business System.[24] That system will help shift the Army's employment paradigm from an almost feudal one to a more collaborative one, from exclusively command directed to increasingly market driven. Perhaps most importantly, it will create as many career paths as the Army has people, which will translate into a richly talented labor force, particularly at the senior officer level.

Differentiating people and capturing that information in an intuitive information system is but part of a holistic talent management system, one focused upon the productive development and employment of every officer. Most importantly, it enables the creation of individual career paths, the focus of Chapter 5.

ENDNOTES - CHAPTER 4

1. Bill Conaty and Ram Charan, *The Talent Masters*. New York: Crown Business Press, 2010, p. 18.

2. Malcolm Gladwell, "Late Bloomers," *The New Yorker*, October 20, 2008, available from *www.newyorker.com/reporting/2008/10/20/081020fa_fact_gladwell*.

3. Wikipedia, *Biography of Harlan Sanders*, available from *en.wikipedia.org/wiki/Colonel_Sanders*.

4. Kate Linebaugh, "The New GE Way: Go Deep, Not Wide," *The Wall Street Journal*, March 7, 2012.

5. Casey Wardynski, David S. Lyle, and Michael J. Colarusso, *Towards a U.S. Army Officer Corps Strategy for Success: Evaluating Talent*, Paper presented at the 47th Annual U.S. Army Senior Conference, West Point, NY, June 2010, p. 197.

6. Over the years, promotion board Memoranda of Instruction have stressed the importance of abilities in governance, geopolitical environment, cultural sensitivity, statesmanship, enterprise management, etc., all virtually impossible to assess by a board, given the information available to it. As a result, analysis prepared by the Army G1 revealed that despite such guidance, there has been no measurable change in promotion board behavior or outcomes. See *Report to the Military Leadership Diversity Commission, Promotion Selection Boards*, Washington, DC: HQDA, DCS G1, December 2009, pp. 5-9.

7. On the eve of the Civil War, for example, George McClellan had a tremendous cumulative advantage over Ulysses Grant. An engineer, McClellan had been second in his West Point class, was author of the Army's cavalry manual, inventor of its standard horse saddle, and president of the Ohio and Mississippi Railroad. Grant, meanwhile, was a quartermaster officer who had resigned his commission in 1854 under threat of court martial, reportedly for intoxication. Since that time, civilian success had eluded him. As a result, in 1861, McClellan was commissioned as a Regular Army major general while Grant was made an Illinois militia colonel.

8. General Carter Ham, Commanding General, U.S. Africa Command (AFRICOM) interview with authors, West Point, NY, October 2011.

9. Hugo Baron von Freytag-Loringhoven, "The Power of Personality in War," *The Roots of Strategy, Vol. 3*, Mechanicsburg, PA: Stackpole Books, 1991, p. 328.

10. Walter R. Mahler, *The Succession Planning Handbook for the Human Resource Executive*, Midland Park, NJ: Mahler Publishing Company, 1986, p. 257.

11. For more on this subject, see the authors' *Accessing Talent: the Foundation of a U.S. Army Officer Corps Strategy*, Carlisle, PA: Strategic Studies Institute, U.S. Army War College, February 2010.

12. We believe that Career Crossroad 2 (the branching process) is an ideal place to pilot the IDEA concept and a supporting talent management information system, ensuring each officer is placed upon an optimal pathway for success. The Army is currently piloting a new branching paradigm at West Point which will eventually scale to the other commissioning sources. It draws heavily upon the concepts we describe here.

13. Major's rank thus becomes a powerful signal—the officer is credentialed as a full practitioner of the Army profession, someone who is not only an expert but also who can **create and impart new professional knowledge** to others.

14. While everyone has talent, some people simply are not suited to the Army profession.

15. Realistic, Investigative, Artistic, Social, Enterprising, and Conventional (RIASEC) types are derived from psychologist John Holland's theory of career choice. It posits that personalities seek out and flourish in the work environments they fit. There is a substantial body of evidence showing a correlation between RIASEC type, job type, and employee performance.

16. They will not be analogous with today's enlisted career counselors, who have a short-term reenlistment focus.

17. Ironically, today there is only one time in an officer's career when the Army provides anything akin to comprehensive, professional career counseling—during the transition from military to civilian life.

18. For example, NBCC administers the National Counselor Examination needed to become a National Certified Counselor.

19. This 2x2 figure is derived from the most widely accepted model for modern HR, presented by Dave Ulrich, *Human Resource Champions*, Boston, MA: Harvard Business School Press, 1997.

20. Transformational HR teams at top enterprises have been using similar assessment matrices for almost 3 decades to map the intersection of an employee's performance (vertical axis) and potential (horizontal axis).

21. Recall that IDEAs reveal much more about an individual than their operational acumen. They do so by gathering granular information on an officer's developmental capacities and experiences gained both inside **and** outside the Army: hobbies, interests, goals, education, personal networks, volunteer work, travel, previous employment, learning style and temperament, native intelligences, etc. The fullness of each officer's life experiences gives him or her unique productive capacities that can be leveraged and extended — **if** the Army is aware of them.

22. Notice that Individual Development and Employment Assessments and subsequent career plans would focus not upon promotion, but upon **productivity** — how best to develop and employ each individual so that collectively, the Army is more effective in realizing its goals. That is the sea change.

23. Hedonic demand theory suggests that the market will reveal information about the true object of demand through the supply and demand mechanism. It disaggregates talent into its constituent characteristics in an effort to determine the contributory value of each characteristic. In other words, it is the demand for the characteristic, not the demand for the individual **possessing** the characteristic, which reveals the valuable information.

24. At the time we write this, that system is slated to be the Integrated Personnel and Pay System-Army with a talent management module scheduled for release sometime after mid-decade.

CHAPTER 5

CREATE RELEVANT EXPERTISE WITH INDIVIDUAL CAREER PATHS

> ... there are many people who have the potential ... to be great ... that never have the opportunity or the training for the full development of their talents.[1]
>
> General Dwight D. Eisenhower

Lieutenant General Patricia Horoho commands the U.S. Army's Medical Command and is also its Surgeon General, the first nurse and woman to serve as top medical officer. It is a compelling story, made more so when considering that Horoho was promoted directly from colonel to major general in 2008 to lead the Army Nurse Corps.

Does this augur a wider return to "Marshall-like" talent management, one where the right officer is selected for the work and given the commensurate rank to do it, regardless of seniority? No. In fact, this type of rapid advancement is common to military nurses—Horoho was the Army's second to skip brigadier general rank, the first being Major General (Retired) Gale Pollock, her predecessor. Her successor, Major General Jimmie Keenan, is the third. The Air Force has skipped head nurses over brigadier general rank as well.

What these promotions do tell us, however, is that deviating from lock-step career paths, with a focus upon talent rather than time in grade, **is** possible, provided that talent and its demand are clearly evident. In the case of nurses, healthcare experts rather than land combat experts, it is easier to differentiate them from other officers, even within the current personnel management system. This may, in part, explain why Army leaders are now comfortable bumping nurses from colonel directly to major general—their clear talents make it a low risk proposition.[2] Unlike many other general officer positions, medical service assignments are not viewed as within the capabilities of MFE officers. If they were, a future corps commander would perhaps be chief nurse today.

If that prospect seems preposterous, consider that many senior officer positions requiring equally specialized expertise (in financial comptrollership, public affairs, force management, logistics, acquisitions, research and development, information technology, human resources, contracting, etc.) are today filled by MFE officers and will be for the foreseeable future. Some of these senior officers possess the functional expertise needed for their jobs. Some do not, however, and as we have pointed out, they will have little opportunity to learn on the job because they are treated as itinerant laborers by an up-or-out management system that often moves them to the next job before they can master the strategic work at hand (see Figure 5-1).

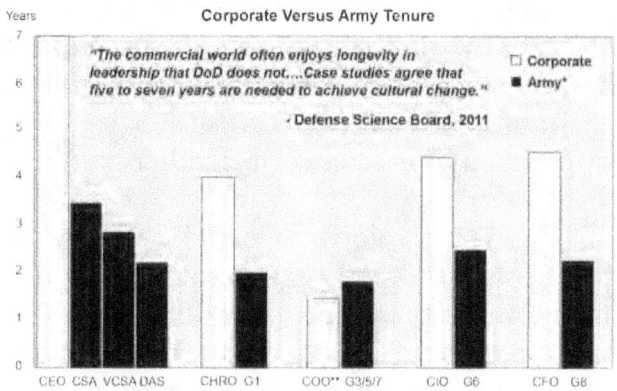

*1991-2011 ** COO positions are declining within Fortune 500 as duties increasingly migrate to CEOs COO positions are often used to onboard rising executives into the C-suite for follow-on jobs

Figure 5-1. Army Staff Principal Churn, 1990-2011.[3]

In the Army, experts such as nurses can usually follow their bliss, moving through a series of assignments that tend to deepen both technical expertise and leadership and management acumen. Relying a last time upon Horoho to make a point, consider that as the commander of Army Medical Command (MEDCOM) she administers a budget of $13.5 billion and manages 480 facilities and 140,000 employees serving more than 3.5 million healthcare beneficiaries in the third largest U.S. healthcare system.[4] Leading that effort requires more than nursing savvy, but a quick review of Horoho's resume shows that each career crossroad has afforded her opportunities to build relevant medical, leadership, and management expertise via a powerful and appropriate mix of developmental and educational opportunities. Barring unforeseen circumstances, she will also have 4 years of assignment tenure. If she fails as the Army's top medical officer, it will not be because her career path failed to prepare her.

By comparison, a senior infantry or armor officer who moves rapidly from Supreme Headquarters Allied Powers Europe Executive Officer to U.S. Army Forces, U.S. European Command G3 and Chief of Staff, then to command a Training and Doctrine Command (TRADOC) Center/School, and finally to the Army G1 for 2 years labors under a tremendous disadvantage when he reaches the Pentagon. Even if an ideal people manager by temperament, intellect, and instinct; even if an adept and inspirational leader; and even if he extracts every bit of relevant expertise from his previous experience and education, this is not his world. It is a world of constant national media scrutiny, Capitol Hill testimony, and budget wars; of powerful personal networks and fuzzy lines of authority. It requires an understanding of job markets and behavioral economics, of civil-military relations, statecraft, and American politics. The officer's previously demonstrated operational adaptability will be sorely challenged within this new environment, one where leading change requires both time and HR expertise, and he has little of either.

Managing senior officers this way is not in the best interest of individuals or the institution, yet for several reasons, the Army continues doing so. First, it is due to bureaucratic muscle memory—it has more or less been done this way since 1947. Second, the Defense Officer Personnel Management Act (DOPMA) and Titles 10 and 37 of the U.S. Code reinforce these management tendencies.[5] Third, a reward culture is in operation, causing leaders to advance well-performing officers into available senior positions even if they are an uncertain match for the work required. Fourth, when officers enter the senior officer ranks as colonels, the Army has little idea how it will employ them several years later, so it cannot take steps to prepare each accordingly. Finally, because evaluation mechanisms such as the current Officer Evaluation Report (OER) reveal little unique or granular information about people, the Army cannot differentiate between them.

With a little foresight, however, the Army can do a better job. By this, we mean creating individual career paths that, coupled with deep succession planning, ensure officers in key assignments always perform optimally. To accomplish this, each officer's career path must navigate the competing demands for both current and future productivity.

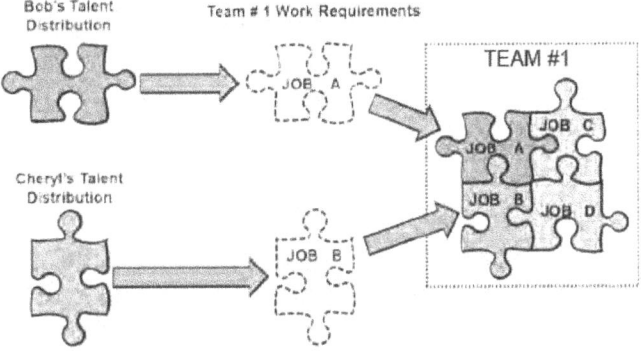

Figure 5-2. Workforce Talent Management for Current Productivity.

For example, in Figure 5-2 we see two senior officers, Bob and Cheryl. Based upon their unique talent distributions, each occupies different talent pools. Meanwhile, Team #1 has been failing and needs two new members. The vacancies support a high risk area and must be filled by optimal performers—the jobs have been designated as **key assignments**. Because the team leader knows exactly the talents demanded by each job, and because the Army knows exactly the talents Bob and Cheryl possess, they are assigned to the jobs they fit best (imagine the consequences of assigning them to the same team but the wrong positions). Both will further develop as a result of their new work experiences, but their assignment to Team #1 was predicated upon the need for **current** productivity from both. Critical to that productivity are behaviors and team fit. If Bob and Cheryl cannot collaborate comfortably with one another, as well as with the existing members of their team, productivity may actually decline rather than rise.

While talent matching for current productivity would be an improvement in officer management, the Army must do more. With an intimate understanding of each officer's unique potential, it can make assignments that, while requiring an appropriate level of performance, provide an opportunity to extend or acquire talents for **future** employment. As Figure 5-3 illustrates, Joe and Sue are unlikely to perform optimally when first assigned to Team #2—they possess the requisite talents to start work, but they must hone existing skills and acquire new ones to reach optimal performance. As the jobs in Team #2 are **not** key billets, sufficient rather than optimal performance is initially acceptable.

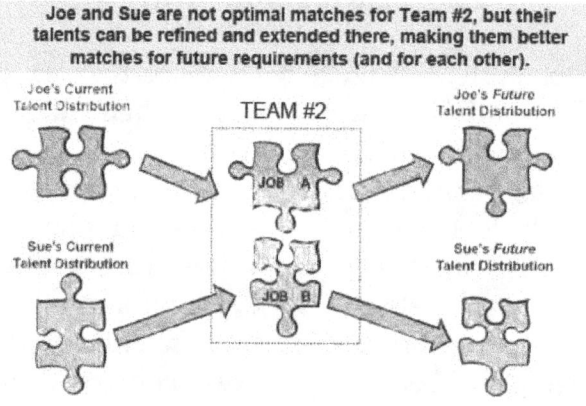

Figure 5-3. Workforce Talent Management for Future Productivity.

The career of Air Force Vice Chief of Staff William McKee helps illustrate these concepts. Like many officers of the "Greatest Generation," General McKee's career had George Marshall's fingerprints on it. McKee is not particularly famous, even in Air Force circles, perhaps because he took a different career path to the top. Usually Air Force senior generals were combat veterans, former pilots, or at least navigators (air crews being analogous to the Army's combat arms). But McKee was a U.S. Army coastal artillerist, not an aviator.

A 1929 West Point graduate, during the interwar years, McKee capably commanded coastal batteries in the Philippines, Puerto Rico, and the United States. But it was in 1935, while stationed at Fort MacArthur, CA, that some previously hidden talents were revealed. During that posting, McKee also served as executive officer of the Civilian Conservation Corps (CCC) in the Los Angeles area. The CCC was an immense New Deal public work relief program for unemployed, military-age men during the Great Depression. At its height, it enrolled over half a million members nationwide. Given its size and composition, the Roosevelt administration initially turned to the Army to run the program. With the Los Angeles area CCC, McKee earned a reputation as a problem solver, talented administrator, and logistician.

After the CCC, McKee returned to the coastal artillery, but in 1942, Marshall transferred him to the U.S. Army Air Forces (AAF) because its Chief, Lieutenant General Hap Arnold, needed an able logistician. After a quick turn in the AAF's Air Defense Directorate (a low-risk on-boarding assignment), he went on to become Deputy Chief of Air Staff for Operations (a key billet) and then commanding general of Air Transport Command (a key billet). From 1953 to 1962, he served successively as Vice Commander and Commander of Air Materiel Command before his culminating assignment as Air Force Vice Chief of Staff.

McKee's career is a good example of managing an officer after identifying his talents and liberating them with a unique career path that maximized his potential. In assessing his abilities, his superiors looked beyond the narrow scope of his artillery duties, identified him as a stellar logistician, gave him the appropriate mix of developmental assignments to shape him for the future, and employed him to best effect without letting policy or tradition constrain his talents. McKee may have lacked the imprimatur of a pilot or combat air crewman, but that was not what the Air Force needed in its Vice Chief in 1962, as Chief of Staff Curtis LeMay already embodied those characteristics. LeMay needed someone to complement his talents, not replicate them.[6]

This type of thoughtful career management is obviously possible, even more so given the advent of Information Age technologies that allow organizations to truly understand their people and work requirements. It is also necessary, not just for organizational effectiveness, but also because today's enormously competitive labor market gives educated professionals the option of seeking new employment whenever a company fails to give them sufficient voice in their work. The industrial era, during which "bosses" unilaterally made employment decisions, is over. As Bruce Tulgan notes in *Winning the Talent Wars:*

> The very best people are least likely to follow the old-fashioned career path . . . in the new economy because they simply don't have to. Their options in the free talent market are endless. And they know it.[7]

In short, the Army needs as many career paths as it has officers if it hopes to get maximum productivity from each over a lifetime of service.

INDIVIDUAL CAREER PATHS

For years, Army HR has tried to introduce "flexible" officer career timelines (usually with the encouragement of successive Chiefs of Staff). In this context, flexible has meant incremental adjustments to the timing and sequence of universally required career gates rather than creating individual career paths for each officer. As HR leaders wrestle with the issue, an oft-stated complaint is that Army requirements pose the chief obstacle to flexible careers. Of course, the bigger constraints are culture, policy, and practice.

Figure 5-4 reveals just how crowded the typical career timeline has become. Today the heart and soul of an officer's career is clearly experiential, with a multitude of key developmental assignments predominating, while Professional Military Education (PME) and civilian education have become peripheral. Evidence for this is the timing of each PME opportunity, which routinely occurs much later in an officer's career than in years past and subsequently has decreasing utility (or, in the case of civilian graduate education, is falling by the wayside entirely, something we'll examine in greater detail in Chapter 6).

Certainly, some of this is due to factors outside of the Army's control—deferments due to joint/manning requirements in wartime, for example. The question, however, is whether "education as afterthought" has become the new normal. Consider the example of a talented officer, continuously deferred from Senior Service College attendance due to strategic-level Army or joint assignments taking her beyond her 25th year of commissioned service. Through no fault of her own, she is now ineligible to attend. Because she has failed to achieve the required military education level (Military Education Level 1/Joint Professional Military Education II), she is eliminated from consideration for general officer promotion.[8]

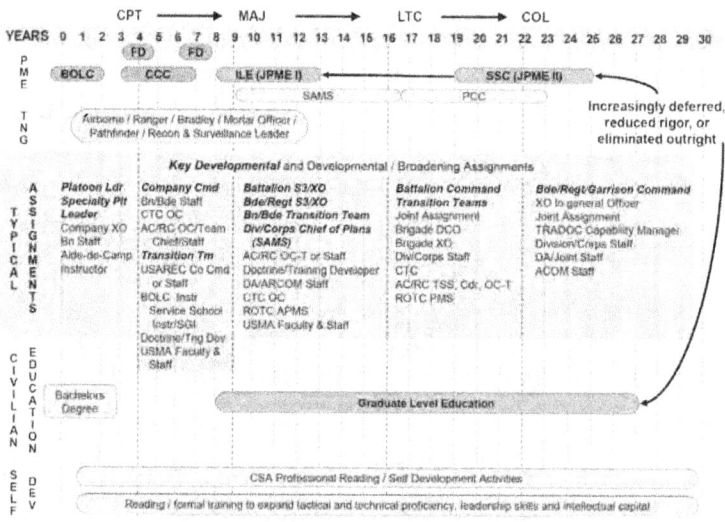

Figure 5-4. *Department of the Army Pamphlet 600-3, Active Duty Infantry Officer Career Timeline.*[9]

To solve this problem, the Army should not create flexible career paths but **unique** ones, tailored experiences that leave room for professional non-negotiables such as timely, relevant continuing education. However, because it really does not know its people, it cannot manage them this thoughtfully. Instead, the Army ensures officers travel similar career paths as a risk management measure, a woefully inefficient practice. As Figure 5-5 demonstrates, the aim is to churn out senior officers with roughly identical capabilities—the "round-peg-in-square-hole" approach.

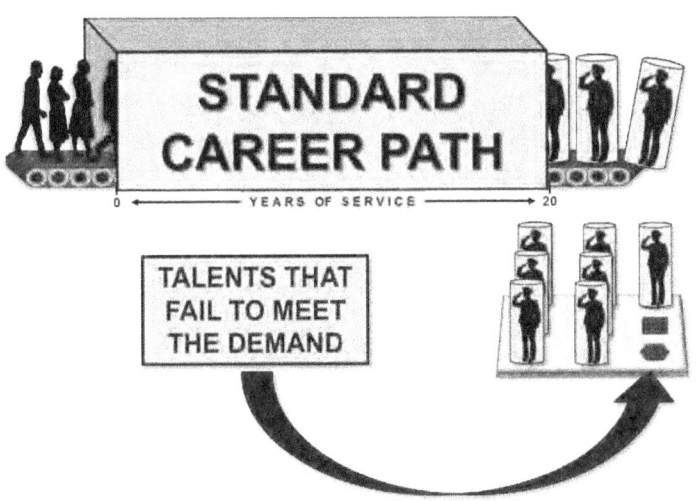

Figure 5-5. Standardized Career Paths Inhibit Differentiation.

Some may respond that uniform development is called for in a uniformed service. If that creates repetitive or unnecessary experiences for some officers, so be it—more experience, education, or training is good, not bad. But this contradicts a fundamental tenet of human capital theory. People develop productive capacities at their own pace, the result of dozens of contributing factors unique to each (different challenges, preferences, experiences, education, peers, innate abilities, etc.). More is not always better because learning resources and capacities are always limited—corner solutions are not the answer.[10] Officers must instead collaborate with the Army to decide which employment and development they need and which they can forego.

As Figure 5-6 illustrates, this entails trade-offs, with each officer moving down a unique career path from mid-career forward. This is the best way to mitigate risk, to ensure the Army possesses the full range of senior officer talents needed to meet the demands of an uncertain future. When thoughtful trade-offs are not made, however, risk rises rather than falls. As a senior allied officer put it:

> At least 10 of my 30-plus years of full-time service, if not more, were spent doing things for which I was demonstrably ill-prepared in terms of both education and experience.... In retrospect it all seems a little amateurish—much time spent training for things I never did and much time spent doing things for which I was never trained.[11]

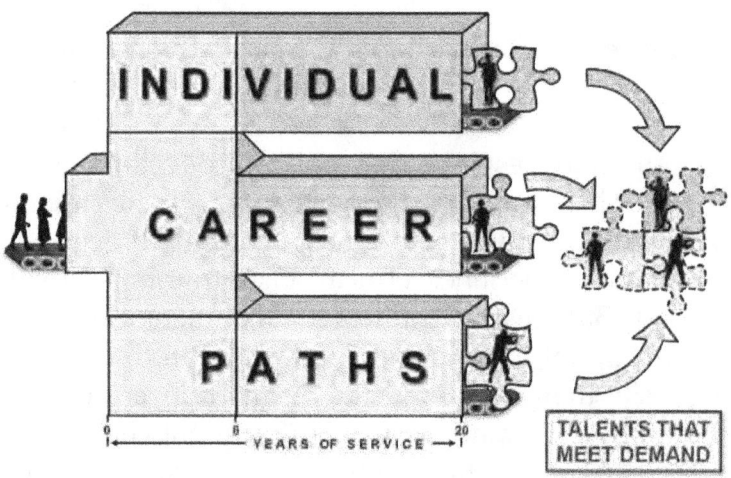

Figure 5-6. Individual Career Paths Foster Talent Differentiation.

To help us think about trade-offs in the current officer management system, consider Figures 5-7 and 5-8. Figure 5-7 represents the notional career path of a senior "Operations" officer (MFE), Figure 5-8 of a senior "Institutional Support" officer (Adjutant General). In both figures, the vertical axis shows three domains:

Cognitive Ability, **Institutional Acumen**, and **Land Combat Expertise**, each subdivided by low, moderate, or high ability for a senior officer. The horizontal axis depicts typical assignments through 30 years of service, as well as career crossroads (2 thru 8).

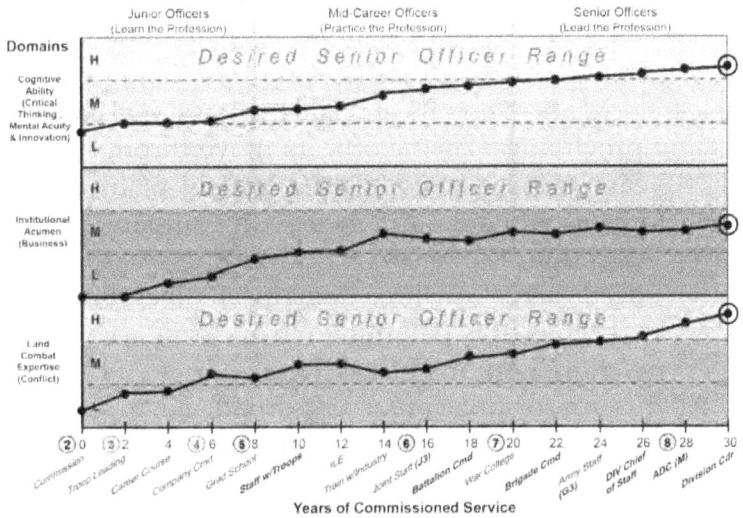

Figure 5-7. Operations (MFE) Career Path.

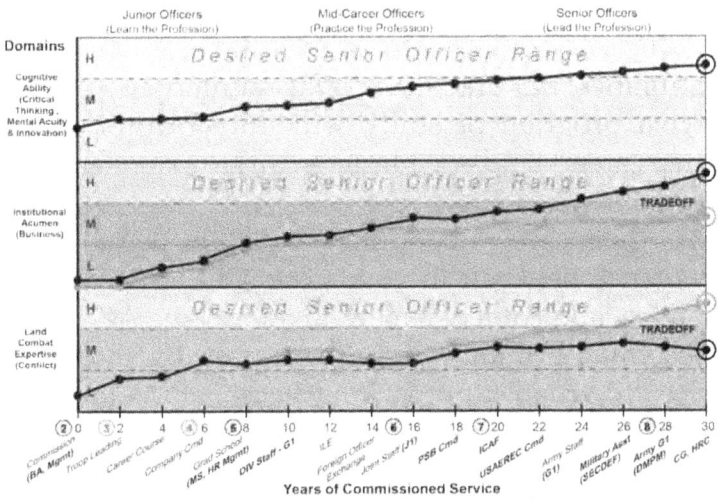

Figure 5-8. Institutional Support (Adjutant General or AG) Career Path.

In our examples, let us assume that both officers possess comparable abilities for advanced cognitive development, as well as the physical fitness, character, and values central to the Army profession. From commissioning, we see little difference between the two other than a slight "institutional acumen" bump for the AG officer based upon her bachelor's degree in management, evidence that pre-commissioning career choices correlate to an officer's later professional capacities and proclivities. As the officers move through their first 8 years of service, comprised largely of division-and-below assignments leavened with company grade officer education, they seem to develop at reasonably similar speeds across all three domains. By their 8th year of service, each is fully committed to an Army career, an expert practitioner of the profession.

At this important career crossroad, each also attends graduate school. The MFE officer's overarching goal is to sharpen his cognitive abilities. Because no civil institution offers a "Master's of Land Combat," he instead chooses Military History, Political Science, an MBA, or perhaps even English or Philosophy. The AG officer is equally interested in honing her cognitive abilities, but unlike her MFE counterpart, she can select a program of study with direct applicability to her career field—a Master's in Human Resource Management.

As their careers continue, we begin to see some divergence between the two. The MFE officer is becoming a land combat expert. Likewise, the AG officer is becoming a human resource expert. By their next career crossroad (approaching lieutenant colonel), it is clear that, while both are agile thinkers, the MFE officer has developed significantly greater land combat talents, while the AG officer has become equally adept in the institutional realm. Figure 5-8 captures the trade-offs—by the time they are major generals, the AG officer will be sorely challenged as the leader of a large maneuver formation but far better prepared to become an Army Staff principal than her MFE counterpart. The way senior officers are managed today, however, it is just as likely (perhaps even more likely) that the MFE officer will become the next Army G1.

To be clear, there's nothing wrong with MFE officers serving as G1, G8, etc., on staffs from division to Army level. If they are going to work in those specialized domains, however, the Army must provide them with a mix of assignments and development providing at least foundational expertise, and only when the officer's preferences and talents suit them for productive work in those domains, not as part of some misguided "broadening" effort.[12] These officers must also have sufficient job tenure, as well as stable staffs with the requisite domain expertise to augment their own.

The current officer management culture routinely accepts tremendous risk, however, by shoving career "operators" into the deep end of the institutional pool to see if they can swim. The prevailing thinking seems to be that leadership risk cannot be accepted in the operating force because such risk has life or death implications. Yet in echelon-above-corps or Army Pentagon assignments, such risk is apparently more acceptable.

Too often, many highly technical staff positions are viewed as good "broadening" assignments for operators who rotate through them so rapidly that they derive limited developmental benefit, and desired strategic outcomes become almost impossible to achieve.[13] In our view, this is at least as risky as selecting the wrong brigade combat team or division commander. Leadership failure at the institutional level has tremendous national security implications, can impact the well-being of all soldiers and their families, and takes much longer to remedy. It can result in dozens of operational units without the appropriate equipment or resources to meet the enemy. In other words, the Army cannot risk failure in any key senior leader positions, whether operational or institutional.

The Army is aware of these challenges and has taken some steps to ameliorate them. For example, at the front end of the Officer Personnel Management System (OPMS), some officers receive a "functional area designation" by their 7th year of commissioned service. The intent is to identify young officers for future development and service in a range of specialties, including Public Affairs, Information Operations, Force Management, Comptrollership, Strategic Plans and Policy, Operations Research, etc.

There are three challenges to this approach. First, little talent information is currently available to functionally designate officers. Second, even for those placed in an appropriate career field, one-size-fits-all career paths and restrictive career gates inhibit their development of deep expertise. Third, selection board results continue to signal that nonoperational specialization entails genuine career risk—the challenge of getting these officers into the upper echelons of Army staff and leadership remains.

As we described in Chapter 3, without a fundamental redress of other OPMS policies and practices, many of these officers may encounter barriers to advancement, causing them to leave the Army before entering its senior officer ranks. To that end, in 2007, the Army changed its selection consideration guidance for brigadier general promotion boards. The intent was to promote more officers in smaller, single track functional areas (nonops experts). According to a 2009 report, results were mixed. Selection rates rose for a few low density specialties but flatlined for many others and actually rose for MFE officers.[14]

Such incremental adjustments to the current OPMS amount to little more than rearranging the deck-chairs on the *Titanic*. The best way to create an adaptable senior officer cohort is not via late-career promotion policy changes but with full-career talent management. Early and continuous individual career planning is critical.

INDIVIDUAL CAREER PLANNING

Diligent individual career planning engenders optimal performance. Such planning requires a wealth of information, however. In Chapter 4, we introduced the concept of Individual Development and Employment Assessments (IDEAs). IDEAs provide the data foundation for mapping individual career paths. As we explained, the information revealed during these assessments can easily be maintained in a comprehensive talent management IT system, one used by officers, Army organizations, and HR talent managers. This dynamic information will allow Army career counselors to assess an officer's performance, potential, readiness, and suitability for any position at any point in time. Figure 5-9 illustrates the data elements required for individual career planning:

- **Performance**. Going as far back as his or her pre-commissioning source, each officer has demonstrated both results and expertise to varying degrees. Prior performance is a logical career planning start point, but one the Army rarely looks beyond.

- **Potential.** Personality, interests, and cognitive aptitudes are unique to each individual, framing the speed and depth of future talent development. It is fair to say that the Army (like many employers) knows almost nothing about these aspects of its people. Rectifying this will require not just better information systems but also increased collaboration with all officers, for only they can reveal their goals and motivations.
- **Readiness.** The talents (and talent gaps) of an individual at any point in time help identify the range of future employment options for him or her. When current productivity is desired (a key billet), talents should be heavily weighted in an assignment decision (employ the officer). Conversely, when future productivity is desired, filling talent gaps should be heavily weighted (develop the officer).
- **Suitability.** Performance, potential, and readiness do much to reveal an officer's capabilities, but assessing whether those capabilities match an organization's challenges and culture is the capstone component of individual career planning. As both change dynamically, career decisions must be made thoughtfully, particularly at the senior officer levels. What do we mean? We mean that without an impending global conflict, perhaps Hugh Drum would have been named Army Chief of Staff in 1939. With war looming, however, President Franklin Roosevelt turned to Marshall, believing him more suitable to the challenges of those times.

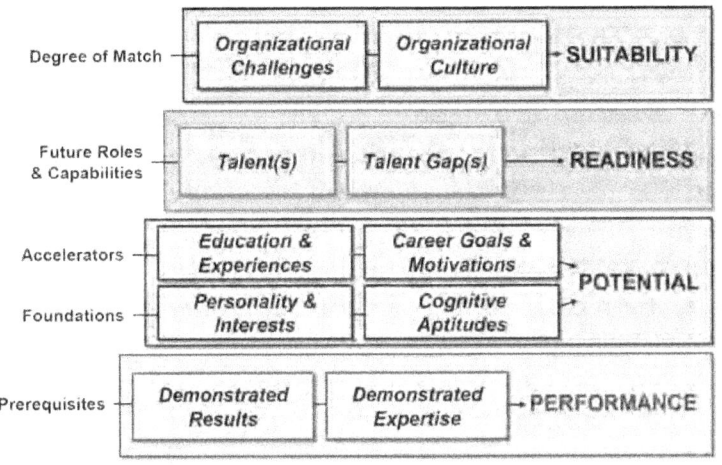

Figure 5-9. Information Required for
Individual Career Planning.[15]

Equipped with accurate, current information on the performance, potential, readiness, and suitability of each officer, the Army will be able to build deep talent pools around the work actually being demanded by its formations and organizations. This information will help break down the silos that often impede officer talent management—binning officers and jobs by rank, year group, career field/functional area, key/developmental assignments, gender, etc. Instead, the Army will rapidly identify the best officer for a particular job in response to the rapidly changing labor requirements of an increasingly complex and uncertain world.

With such granular information, career paths could begin to resemble the model illustrated in Figure 5-10. Notice that it is built around three things: assessment (IDEAs), continuing development (particularly education and credentialing), and then employment (assignments). For ease of execution, IDEAs are aligned with professional military education wherever possible (at Career Crossroads 1, 2, 5, and 7). This is because the schools provide a stable environment in which to conduct penetrating talent assessments of each officer. If sufficiently rigorous, these schools can also serve as excellent screening, vetting, and culling tools. For example, in this career model, both Intermediate Level Education (ILE) and Senior Service College attendance are associated with the retention decision points first discussed in Chapter 3. Part of the retention decision will rest upon whether or not officers meet rigorous entrance standards for graduate-level PME at a staff school or senior service college, as well as their academic performance while enrolled.

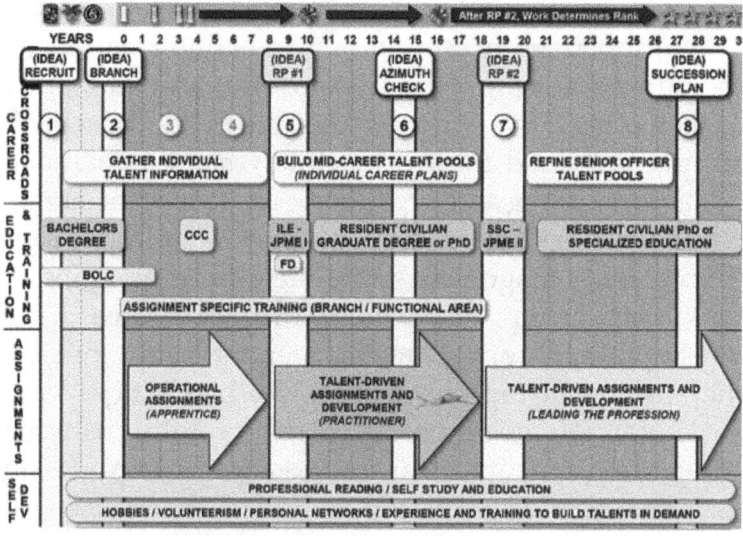

Figure 5-10. Individual Career Path Template.

PME is also aligned with IDEAs/career crossroads so that officers receive the education needed to handle levels of increasing complexity before they are asked to do so, generating a real return on the investment. Consider ILE at the Command and General Staff School at Fort Leavenworth, KS, for example. Upon graduation from a rigorous program of tailored education and assessment, officers would be certified as "full practitioners" of the profession, promotable captains. These officers would then have almost 11 years to "swim" in their respective talent pools, receiving assignment-specific training only as needed and completing a resident civilian graduate degree en route to their next retention point: Career Crossroad 7/Senior Service College. The stultifying collection of "mandatory" career gates would fall by the wayside as officers worked in assignments aligned more directly with their talents.

As the Army uses the right incentives and tools to differentiate both people and work, it will gain a much clearer sense of the talents it must cultivate via individual career paths. As it collects that information in a user-friendly talent management information system, it will be better postured to collaborate with its officers in their assignments and development. As this knowledge liberates dollars and people from industrial-era personnel management practices, it will permit the reallocation of fiscal and human resources towards Information Age talent management. A critical component of this new way of managing people is higher and specialized education, integral to individual career planning.

ENDNOTES - CHAPTER 5

1. *Department of the Army Pamphlet 600-65, Leadership Quotes*, Washington, DC: HQ Department of the Army, November 1985, p. 7.

2. In fact, there are no longer brigadier general positions for active duty Army nurses, so this is now common practice. The lesson: an officer need not spend time as a brigadier general if he or she is already prepared to shift to a higher band of responsibility requiring major general's rank. The **work** and the officer's **suitability** for it dictate the rank, not time in service.

3. CEO Tenure, available from *content.spencerstuart.com/ss-website/pdf/lib/Final_Summary_for_2008_publication.pdf*; CHRO Tenure, available from *chronicle.com/section/Home/5*; COO Tenure, available from *www.entrepreneur.com/tradejournals/article/146747083.html*; CIO Tenure, available from *www.cio.com/article/153600/Average_CIO_Tenure_Slips_But_Still_More_Than_Four_Years*; CFO Tenure, available from *www.financialweek.com/apps/pbcs.dll/article?AID=/20080901/REG/309019973/0/71214020&template=printart*.

4. "Horoho takes oath as first nurse, female surgeon general," December 8, 2011, available from *www.army.mil/article/70556/Horoho_takes_oath_as_first_nurse__female_surgeon_general/*.

5. These govern Armed Forces personnel management and pay and allowances, respectively, which tie compensation directly to seniority.

6. Warren Kozak, *Lemay: The Life and Wars of General Curtis LeMay*, New York: Regnery Publishing, Inc, 2009, p. 336.

7. Bruce Tulgan, *Winning the Talent Wars*, New York: W. W. Norton & Co., 2001, p. 154.

8. Per *Army Regulation 350-1*, theoretically this officer could be granted "constructive credit" for service college attendance by HQDA G3/5/7, although she would still need to achieve JPME II certification certification by attending the National Defense University's 10-week Joint and Combined Warfighting School.

9. Figure 9-1, "The Active Army Infantry Developmental Model," *DA Pam 600-3*, Washington, DC: February 1, 2010.

10. A corner solution is an instance where the outcome being sought (in this case, an adaptable senior officer corps) is based not

upon the market-efficient maximization of related quantities, but instead upon brute-force boundary conditions (such as "we cannot advance a leader without career gate x, y, or z") that put the actual solution (in this case, individual career paths) outside the permitted values.

11. Brigadier (Retired) Nick Jans, *The "Once were Warriors" Syndrome and Strategic Leadership in the Profession of Arms*, Canberra, Australia: Centre for Defence Leadership and Ethics, Australian Defence College, 2011, p. 11.

12. Might the MFE officer in our example possess the innate talents critical to later success as HR leader for an organization with millions of employees? Absolutely. Did the career path in Figure 5-7 sufficiently prepare him for that role? In our judgment, no.

13. While conducting our research, we interviewed several general officers on either the Army Staff or in separate commands. A common refrain was "I don't know why I was selected for this job." Equally common was "By the time I have it figured out, I'll have to move."

14. G1, *2009 Report to the Military Leadership Diversity Commission*, Washington, DC: DCS, p. 12.

15. Concept Source: "Succession Planning and Talent Management," presentation at the 2007 IPMAAC Conference, St. Louis, MO, Personnel Decisions International Ninth House, slide 62.

CHAPTER 6

INVEST IN HIGHER AND SPECIALIZED EDUCATION

> If you are thinking one year ahead, plant rice. If you are thinking 10 years ahead, plant trees. If you are thinking a hundred years ahead, educate your people.
>
> Chinese Proverb

> An educated man can experience more in a day than an uneducated man in a lifetime.
>
> Seneca

Chairman of the Joint Chiefs of Staff Martin Dempsey is an avid reader and writer, a general who exercises genuine thought leadership through frequent presentations and publications.[1] While his penchant for communication is perhaps unsurprising (he possesses a Master's degree in literature from Duke University), such "public deep thinking" is increasingly uncommon among senior Army officers. In many respects, Dempsey is a throwback to the post-Vietnam era of intellectuals such as William Depuy, Donn Starry, Paul Gorman, and Max Thurman, generals committed to continuous learning, innovation, and reinvention.

General Dempsey is viewed by many as the senior officer archetype for today's complex world—a talented polymath, equally comfortable leading a division-level command against Iraqi insurgents or imagining the Army's future at Training and Doctrine Command (TRADOC). The general himself, however, often points out that his success across a spectrum of complex challenges is in large part due to the interdisciplinary experts he surrounds himself with, officers as different from him as they are from one another. Such diversity of expertise is the product of several factors, education being chief among them. The military readily acknowledges that education:

> ... develops habits of mind applicable to a broad spectrum of endeavors....[it] is largely defined through the cognitive domain and fosters breadth of view, diverse perspectives, critical analysis, abstract reasoning, comfort with ambiguity and uncertainty, and innovative thinking, particularly with respect to complex, non-linear problems.[2]

An Army officer's education begins with an undergraduate degree and continues after commissioning. That continuing education can take place inside or outside of the defense establishment, which possesses several graduate degree-granting staff or senior service colleges. These schools focus predominately upon developing ". . . the military professional's expertise in the art and science of war."[3] As one command recently noted, however, "The complexity of the future suggests that the education of senior officers must not remain limited to staff and war colleges, but should extend to the world's best graduate schools."[4] We agree. Just as most American universities seek graduate students and faculty from other institutions, the Army, too, should avoid insular educational practices. This is important for several reasons.

First, while the senior service colleges certainly hone more than expertise in the "art and science of war," their 10-month programs are no substitute for the specialized education provided to students in America's top graduate schools. There is no shame in this—each type of institution offers critical but complementary professional education. Civilian graduate degree programs vary substantially from the service colleges in length, content, and pedagogy. Collectively, these programs better develop the body of knowledge essential to a senior officer's expertise in the art and science of institutional leadership and management (economics, history, society, culture, religion, civil-military relations, law and dissent, statecraft, American politics, geopolitics, technology, innovation, strategic communications, financial and human resource management, etc.).

Second, the Army routinely leverages the strengths of the nation to gain advantage over potential adversaries, and leaving the benefits of American higher education on the table is simply not an option—such education gives the senior officer corps a far deeper and broader intellectual bench. Certainly global competitors such as the Chinese recognize this.[5] According to the Institute of International Education, China is the number one source of international students in U.S. universities, with over 157,000 in academic year 2010-11.[6] Some of these students are officers of the People's Liberation Army (PLA), which is dramatically expanding the role of civilian universities in its officer education programs.[7] As early as 2000, the PLA annually had more officers attending American graduate schools than the U.S. military did.[8]

Third, given the breakneck pace of global change, world-class continuing education is more important than ever before. As we have previously mentioned, knowledge becomes dated more rapidly now than at any time in human history. Continuous learning is a critical success trait for contemporary leaders, whether in the military, government, or private sector. To be truly effective, however, education must be rigorous. Top-tier graduate programs make far greater demands upon students, pushing them out of their intellectual comfort zones in a way that the service colleges simply do not.

Finally, and perhaps most importantly:

> [Civilian] graduate education has a decidedly positive impact on professional competence, prestige, and leadership qualities, while reinforcing civilian control and democratic values; it must become an integral part of the professional career — not tangential.[9]

In other words, graduate school refreshes the officer corps' connection to the thoughts, hopes, aspirations, and innovations of the society it serves. In the volunteer force era, this is critically important to the maintenance of healthy civil-military relations.

These benefits are routinely acknowledged in joint and Army doctrinal literature. Given such seeming commitment, why then is officer higher education a topic of concern among current and retired Army, Department of Defense (DoD), and congressional leaders? Perhaps it is because mounting evidence suggests the officer corps has skewed toward action and away from intellect, that a rising generation of senior officers lacks continuing educational opportunity, and that there is increasingly poor alignment between officer education and the demands of the future. Left unchecked, these trends may have serious national security implications.

SENIOR OFFICER GRADUATE EDUCATION TRENDS

There is some evidence that pursuing civilian graduate education entails significant career risk for an officer. For example, Figure 6-1 indicates that future senior leaders are increasingly a product of the DoD's PME in-house graduate schools only. Chart A shows that almost 80 percent of separating lieutenant colonels and colonels possess a civilian graduate degree, with roughly half of these from fully funded, resident attendance at civilian universities. Meanwhile, Chart B shows that by 2010, only 31 percent of all brigadier generals possessed a resident civilian graduate degree, down from almost 54 percent in 1995.

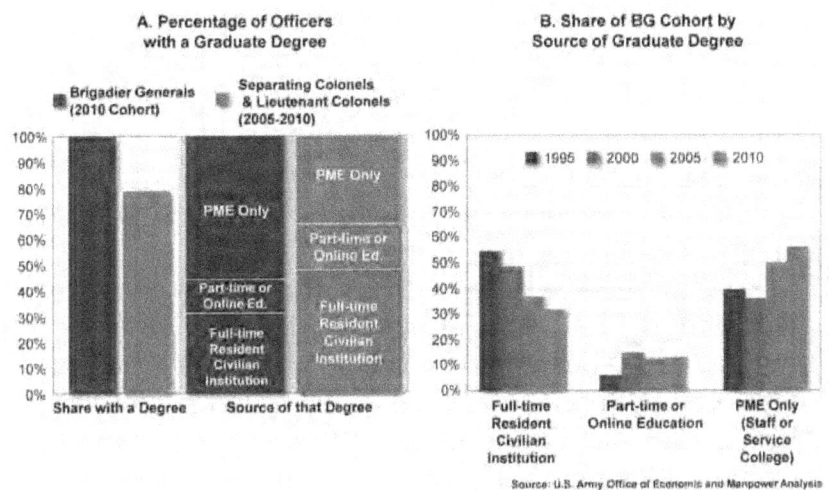

Figure 6-1. Senior Officer Graduate Education Trends, 1995-2010.

It would be easy to ascribe these shifts to the demands of wartime, a "run to the guns" that made higher education a temporary casualty among senior officers. The data do not support that conclusion, however. The situation stems instead from a dramatic reduction in graduate education opportunities during the Army's post-Cold War drawdown (dropping from 5,500-7,000 annual slots in the mid-1980s to less than 400 by 1995).[10] Current doctrinal pronouncements notwithstanding, the Army turned away from officer higher education a full decade before September 11, 2001.

With fewer opportunities for graduate school, and with general officer promotions increasingly awarded to those with senior service college and distance learning degrees only, career-minded officers concluded that attending civilian graduate school entailed great career risk while providing little career benefit.[11] Time spent in a civilian school (often coupled with a follow-on utilization tour) took officers away from jobs that could make them more competitive for promotion — why risk it when the School of Advanced Military Studies or a service college could check the Masters Degree block?

Within the last decade, the Army has taken some steps to reemphasize graduate education. For example, Army Secretary Francis Harvey and Chief of Staff General Pete Schoomaker instituted the officer Career Satisfaction Program (CSP) in 2006. For those commissioned in that year or later, the program provides graduate school opportunities for hundreds of promotable captains annually, without a post-school utilization tour.[12] As a result, upon graduation, these officers can immediately apply their new knowledge and intellectual acumen wherever the Army needs it.

This program, however, which harvests thousands of man-years of service at nominal cost while simultaneously creating longer-serving, more productive mid-career officers, is routinely threatened with cancellation. Perhaps that is because the decline in Army graduate education has created an officer culture that does not value it. As former Secretary of Defense Robert McNamara once said, "Brains are like hearts . . . they go where they're appreciated."[13] Organizations that deemphasize educational credentials cause those who value education to seek it elsewhere and engender anti-intellectualism among many who remain.

These developments run counter to present-day demands for adaptable officers. Adaptability stems from developmental programs that place people in unfamiliar situations and require them to figure things out. Civilian graduate education is a proven way to develop mental agility and adaptability. In fact, because education teaches people **how** to think, it prepares them to devise solutions and responses beyond that which is rote or rule based and helps them to extract greater knowledge from experience and training.[14]

For almost 2 decades, however, the signal to the officer corps has been loud and clear: civilian graduate education is not critical to the Army profession. As a result, future senior officers possess less civilian education than their predecessors, a trend that is continuing. Many of them will lead the Army without the specialized expertise needed in a world that increasingly demands data-enabled decisionmaking, deep knowledge of institutional and governmental dynamics, thought leadership from outside the narrow confines of the Army or DoD, and an emphasis upon managerial disciplines and talents. While some of these officers will manage to succeed, an increasing number may not.

CHALLENGES AT THE SENIOR SERVICE COLLEGES

General Robert Cone, commander of TRADOC, is "truly disturbed" by officer education trends. As he says, "Our Army has been successful because of the rich tradition of intellectualism in our operational culture. . . . They are deeply entwined."[15] But he points out that today there is a serious divide between the two, one manifested not just by reduced senior officer civil schooling, but also by a general disdain for Army schoolhouse assignments or attendance. This growing anti-intellectualism is affecting the entire officer education system, to include the senior services colleges.

Undue reliance upon the senior service colleges as Masters Degree-conferring institutions is a poor strategy, and not just for reasons already discussed. Observers have recently noted several challenges to their efficacy, even in their centerpiece role as inculcators of strategic military art and science expertise. One professor at the U.S. Army War College (USAWC) argues that most officers care more about selection than attendance. He points to Army Force Generation centric systems, procedures, and philosophy as the main culprits in creating a culture that views attendance as an onerous requirement, more of a distraction than an investment in the Army's future. Citing a deferral rate that has averaged 50 percent over the last 5 years, the professor says class composition has shifted from "students with good reason to attend" to "those merely available to attend."[16]

Another USAWC faculty member says the culture of deferment is quite real and negatively affects students, staff, faculty, and thus the tenor of academic discourse:

> There are a number of students attending the war colleges who should not be there, and who really do not want to be there. They want the block checked for their next assignment and promotion. *They can skate through, meeting minimal requirements*, contributing to a form of ignorance on fire by waxing philosophical in seminar dialogue without conducting assigned reading, and enjoy the myriad social experiences that take place beyond the classroom. There is very little in place to prevent such freeloading.[17]

That intellectual "freeloading," according to an Air War College faculty alumnus and current Naval War College professor, is due in part to a service school pedagogy that eschews rigor, permits counterproductive familiarity between instructors and students, and handcuffs faculty to a "moderator" rather than "teacher" role:

> First . . . never use red ink grading student papers: direct criticism of military professionals would be insulting. Second, never cold call a student: not knowing the answer would be demeaning. Third, . . . the classroom is for sharing student views, so faculty should speak minimally. This last instruction often resulted in 90-minute sessions where students mostly reinforced each other's views and shared dead wrong information. . . .[18]

Other faculty members have identified lack of academic rigor as a senior service college challenge. In 2011, an Air War College emeritus professor wrote a highly controversial critique of the college that was quickly rebutted by the school's commandant. While many of its arguments are anecdotal, the critique also contains some evidence, noting that one department "gave the grade of 'A' or 'A-' to 97 percent of the students in its core course."[19] It also notes that:

> . . . the Air War College has appended one element to its academic program that is largely unknown to academic graduate institutions: *remediation of course failures*. Students who failed [an] examination (which rarely happens) or who produced unacceptable papers traditionally had the absolute right to re-accomplish the task because the officers are viewed as expensive assets that cannot be allowed to fail. Virtually 100 percent of those who fail the first time pass the second effort.[20]

We, too, believe that the staff and service colleges should adopt a more rigorous pedagogy. Attendance is a terrific opportunity to learn about people and to validate their suitability for future assignments, but only **if** the curriculum truly puts them through their paces, as was the case in the Army during the interwar years. For example, many officers who served in **both** world wars characterized not combat, but their time at the Command and General Staff College (CGSC) as the most mentally taxing of their professional careers:

> The Leavenworth schools in the 1920s and 1930s had a deserved reputation for rigor and hard work. . . . Nearly universal in the memoirs of officers who attended the [2-year] course . . . are discussions of studying until midnight every weeknight and the need to take breaks from the rigor of the course work.[21]

Ernie Harmon, who commanded XXII Corps in Europe during World War II, said the stress of CGSC made him "as mean as a starving prairie wolf, or . . . a cobra without a convenient snake charmer."[22] While attending CGSC, George Patton wrote to his wife that

"I never seem to get through anymore. It is now 11:30 and I have just finished. Either I study harder or the lessons are harder."[23]

As we mentioned in Chapter 5, staff schools and service colleges can and should serve as powerful screening, vetting, and culling tools on the path to senior leadership—there are plenty of officers in the pipeline to replace those who cannot cut it. As with any institution of higher learning, rigorous entrance standards should be upheld to ensure selectees are academically capable of success and to identify specific gaps in each student's knowledge or learning abilities.[24] In particular, previous academic performance should be given significant weight in the student selection process.

Without these screening and vetting mechanisms, no differentiation or culling of senior officers can take place. PME curricula will remain pegged to the abilities of the weakest students to ensure they can make it through the program. Of course, 100 percent graduation rates and "do over" exams drastically reduce the value of the credentials conferred and are another missed opportunity to differentiate people into talent pools (Who are the polished communicators, the deeply analytical thinkers, the consummate researchers, the mathematically inclined, the data-focused problem solvers, etc.?).

If the senior service colleges face particular challenges now, perhaps it is because they are most vulnerable whenever anti-intellectualism holds sway within their services. Consider that a deferment culture will never exist at Columbia or Yale. Students fight to get in, and the benefits of the diploma are unquestioned—one is far more likely to enjoy success with that credential than without it. Civilian universities are in full control of their resource, faculty, and student selection processes, all of which, if properly managed, signal an ongoing commitment to value-producing higher education. At institutions such as the USAWC, however, an external actor (HQDA) influences the cultural and academic environment via policy actions, selects a significant portion of the faculty, and selects all of the students (whether they want to be there or not).

That is why comparisons of the senior service colleges to civilian universities have limited utility. No matter how good their commandants or faculty may be, the service colleges cannot insulate themselves from misguided corporate policies, as they are in fact **corporate** universities.[25] A corporate university's mandate is to provide complementary education to senior executives, not to replace higher education. Its superpower is the ability to link employee learning to organizational strategy and culture as each evolves in response to a dynamic world. Whether or not this linkage exists can only be ascertained via a robust assessment system.

We recommend five assessment areas: student reaction and satisfaction; learning; application of new knowledge; business impact; and return on investment.[26] The first is relatively easy to assess, the last perhaps the most difficult. For the Army, assessment is further complicated by an era of increased "jointness," as more of its officers receive their MEL 1 (Military Education Level) education from service colleges or fellowship institutions beyond its control (for example, at the time we write this, just three of 10 currently serving Army four-stars attended the USAWC).[27]

Given the senior service college assessment challenge, a comprehensive 2010 House Committee on

Armed Services subcommittee report on professional military education is useful. It found that:

> Some operational commanders, including the Combatant Commanders, reportedly consider their staff officers lacking in certain critical abilities necessary to perform their jobs effectively. Significant numbers of officers are serving in staff positions without having appropriate levels of PME prior to assignment. Furthermore, *many officers reportedly consider the PME they receive to be inadequate preparation for these assignments.*[28]

The authors were quick to point out that this was less a result of how the schools operate internally and more a result of how their respective services resource, manage, and employ them.

Two Army-specific concerns from the report merit further discussion. The first was that the Chief of Staff of the Army should "maintain ownership" of the USAWC. Several contributors to the report found the college's subordination to TRADOC troubling. One described TRADOC as an organization ". . . deeply and zealously imbued with the philosophy and culture of **training**" rather than education, which could introduce "excessive service biases" to the USAWC curriculum.[29] Others thought the shift reduced emphasis upon senior officer education by blocking the college commandant's ability to present resource or other challenges directly to the Army Chief of Staff.[30]

A second concern was with the brief leadership tenure provided to service college commandants, described as ". . . erod[ing] the spirit of educational autonomy over time."[31] We, too, find this problematic. The USAWC has had 48 commandants in 89 years of operation—an average duty tour of 1.8 years per commandant.[32] While held responsible for the production of strategic thinkers, commandants are not afforded a strategic leader's timespan of discretion (recall our discussion from Chapter 2). As a result, they are forced to serve as caretakers rather than innovators—their ability to create new value is circumscribed by their truncated assignment tenure. Increasing commandant assignment length to 5 years is something we think the Army and its sister services should do as soon as possible. (We will discuss tenure extensively in Chapter 8.)

Collectively, the senior service colleges comprise the upper tier of a top-flight corporate university system. They exist for sound reasons and are staffed with many excellent officers and scholars—there are perhaps no better places to study the art and science of war. We have highlighted challenges at the colleges not out of a spirit of criticism, but to reinforce our concern with their increasing use as a graduate school substitute. Just as corporations do not rely unduly upon their internal educational systems to provide post-graduate education, neither should the Army. Ten months at a service college does not make a strategic leader. It can certainly burnish the strategic talents of an officer, but it is far more efficacious when coupled with the expertise gained via civilian graduate education, which should be mandatory for all senior officers.

LACK OF SPECIALIZED GENERAL OFFICER EDUCATION

After attending a senior service college or fellowship institution, continuing education opportunities for senior officers virtually end, just as the complexity and specialized nature of their assignments continues to grow. There is, of course, a suite of required courses, varying in length from as little as 4 hours to the 6-week CAPSTONE course taught at the National Defense University, which prepares new generals to work in a joint environment. Other than CAPSTONE, for the most part these courses are of short duration (a week or less). All of them tend to focus upon responsibilities and situations generals may encounter at progressively higher ranks. They are not education in the true sense of the word, but training courses with little academic rigor or specialization. To succeed in assignments for which they may have insufficient expertise, this forces some general officers to rely upon experience (which may be dated or inapplicable), self-study (for which there is little to no time), and personal relationships (often with others possessing similarly dated experience or knowledge).

Specialized education is perhaps more critical at this level than at any other, as mistakes stemming from uninformed decisions may have strategic importance. But because the rapid rotation job model prevails and tenure in key senior officer positions is usually insufficient, specialized education is difficult to plan. Consider a general who is identified to lead an Army staff section because of another officer's sudden retirement or inability to gain confirmation. Once she assumes her duties, she may have 24 months in position before she moves on. She will have no opportunity to receive specialized executive education beforehand, and she can ill afford it after starting her new duties—time is short, and she must demonstrate positive action of some kind. Seeking education is also an acknowledgment that she is not ready for the job, something to be avoided at all costs.

This scenario plays out with some regularity in the Army, due mostly to reliance upon an "up-or-out" system rather than a talent management approach. Even if just one unexpected vacancy occurs, it can immediately lead to several others. Filling a three-star vacancy usually robs a two-star position, which, in turn, vacates a brigadier general position, and so on. Like a pebble in a pond, an unexpected vacancy can ripple across the senior officer ranks, creating personnel churn that stifles both productivity and personal development.[33]

Unfortunately, even if current management practices made it easier to plan for continuing specialized education, none is being offered to generals, which magnifies the importance of building the right senior officers from the point of commissioning. For example, even if time and funding were made available to send the next Army G1 to Cornell University's executive education for Chief Human Resource Officers, a Maneuver Fires and Effects (MFE) officer whose entire professional and academic background lies outside the HR realm might gain far less from the opportunity than another with deep HR domain knowledge and experience.

As we have said, effective talent management entails trade-offs. While ongoing investment in specialized education for senior officers is a must, care must be exercised in its application. A primer in enterprise financial management will probably not make a land combat expert a good G8, but it might make an officer with a financial management background a great G8. While all officers are capable of continued learning, at some point, the Army's "jack-of-all-trades" approach to senior officer management must end. Each senior officer's performance can be optimized if his or her talents are identified early and cultivated over the course of the person's career. Differentiating officers into talent pools is an integral component of effective succession planning, our next focus area.

ENDNOTES - CHAPTER 6

1. For example, from October 2010 to March 2011 alone, General Dempsey published a series of six articles in *Army Magazine* focused upon continuous learning, institutional adaptation, leader development, and the Army profession.

2. Chairman, Joint Chiefs of Staff (CJCS) Instruction, *Officer Professional Military Education Policy,* Washington, DC: CJCS, July 15, 2009, pp. A-1-A-2.

3. *Ibid.*, p. A-A-1.

4. United States Joint Forces Command, *2010 Joint Operating Environment*, Brunssum, Netherlands, p. 70.

5. According to the Institute of International Education, 10 times as many Chinese study in the United States as Americans study in China, and 600 times more Chinese study English than Americans study Mandarin.

6. See *www.iie.org/Research-and-Publications/Open-Doors/Data/International-Students/Leading-Places-of-Origin/2009-11*.

7. Roy Kamphausen, Andrew Scobell, and Travis Tanner, eds., *The "People" in the PLA: Recruitment, Training and Education in China's Military*, Carlisle, PA: Strategic Studies Institute, U.S. Army War College, September 2008, pp. 139-140.

8. United States Joint Forces Command, *2008 Joint Operating Environment*, Brunssum, Netherlands, p. 26.

9. Sam C. Sarkesian and William J. Taylor, Jr., "The Case for Civilian Graduate Education for Professional Officers," *Armed Forces & Society*, January 1, 1975, p. 252.

10. As a result, fewer than one in 10 officers commissioned in the 1990s through 2005 could expect to receive a fully funded graduate school program from the Army. Officer cohorts in this era ranged from 4,000-6,000 per year, and each cohort had roughly 400 fully funded graduate school billets available.

11. As one mid-career officer recently wrote to us,

> I've been at this for 16 years and love the Army. But I've . . . come to realize that the master's degree that the Army paid for, the fellowship I did at a think tank, and memberships in . . . professional organizations mean zilch to the . . . assignments process.

12. CSP is a retention incentive program offered to ROTC and West Point cadets at commissioning. In exchange for 3-4 additional years of active duty as part of their initial military service obligation, they are guaranteed fully funded attendance at the graduate school of their choice, usually after company command but before selection to major. Approximately 600 cadets a year elect the option—their generation is seeking continuous education. At the time we write this, the program is pending cancellation in fiscal year 2014.

13. For an interesting discussion of this anti-intellectualism, see Major General (Retired) Robert H. Scales, "Too Busy to Learn," *U.S. Naval Institute Proceedings*, February 2010, available from *www.usni.org/magazines/proceedings/story.asp?STORY_ID=2195*.

14. In many ways, what occurs in education is akin to spending time in a foreign country. Understanding the customs, behaviors, and viewpoints of others expands one's world view. The more expansive that world view, the easier it is to adapt to new situations and figure things out.

15. Lance Bacon, "General presents his vision for future warriors," October 4, 2011, available from *www.army.mil/article/66696*.

16. Charles D. Allen, "Redress of Professional Military Education: The Clarion Call," *Joint Force Quarterly*, Issue 59, 4th Quarter 2010, pp. 95-98.

17. George E. Reed, "What's Wrong and What's Right with the War Colleges," *DefensePolicy.org*, July 1, 2011, available from *www.defensepolicy.org/2011/george-reed/what%E2%80%99s-wrong-and-right-with-the-war-colleges*. Italics are ours.

18. Joan Johnson-Freese, "Teach Tough, Think Tough: Why Military Education Must Change," *AOL Defense*, June 15, 2011, available from *defense.aol.com/2011/06/15/teach-tough-think-tough/*.

19. Daniel J. Hughes, "Professors in the Colonels' World," in *Military Culture and Education*, Douglas Hightree, ed., London, UK: Ashgate Publishing, 2011, p. 154.

20. *Ibid*. Italics are ours.

21. Peter J. Schifferle, *America's School for War*, Lawrence, KS: University of Kansas Press, 2010, p. 137.

22. *Ibid*.

23. *Ibid*., p. 144.

24. This is standard practice in several military educational systems, to include the Chinese, the British, and some Commonwealth nations.

25. We recognize that the service colleges create and impart warfighting expertise critical to protecting society. This makes them professional institutions, certainly not analogous with Iams or Hamburger University. When we say "corporate university," we are applying Peter Jarvis' generally accepted definition of internal institutions ". . . created for developing and educating employees in order to meet the corporation's purpose . . . [and] designed to respond quickly to corporate needs." See Peter Jarvis, *Universities and Corporate Universities*, Sterling, VA: Stylus Publishing, Inc., 2001.

26. Lance Berger and Dorothy Berger, eds., *The Talent Management Handbook*, New York: McGraw Hill, 2004, p. 203.

27. Fellowships increased from 45 in 2005 to 89 in 2012. In what we view as a positive development, 35 of those were outside of the Department of Defense.

28. *Another Crossroads? Professional Military Education Two Decades after the Goldwater-Nichols Act and the Skelton Panel*, Washington, DC: U.S. House of Representatives, Committee on Armed Services, Subcommittee on Oversight and Investigations, April 2010, p. xiv. Italics are ours.

29. *Ibid.*, p. 105. Emphasis by authors.

30. In an encouraging move, the Army has recently restored the War College's status as a direct reporting unit (DRU) and it is no longer subordinate to TRADOC.

31. *Another Crossroads? Professional Military Education Two Decades after the Goldwater-Nichols Act and the Skelton Panel.*

32. By comparison, West Point has had 58 superintendents in 210 years—an average tenure of 3.6 years per superintendent. Harvard has had 31 presidents in 375 years—an average tenure of 12 years per president.

33. This illustrates the critical relationship between senior officer assignment tenure, succession planning, and education.

CHAPTER 7

IMPROVE SUCCESSION PLANNING

> The common conception of succession planning ... has to do with changing leadership at the top ... [but] ... the bottom of the organization is where succession planning actually starts if organizations really wish to develop their own talent.[1]
>
> Dennis C. Carey,
> Vice-Chairman, U.S. Dayton Ogden

On December 12, 1941, a 51-year old Army colonel was en route to Hawaii to assess the operational and strategic situation in the wake of the Japanese attack at Pearl Harbor. Highly regarded for his intellectual acumen and strategic vision, he was General George Marshall's choice to become the next Chief of War Plans, and a general's star was already in his future. The colonel's B-18 bomber flew from Mitchel Field, NY, to Phoenix, AZ, for a short stopover, departing quickly for San Francisco, CA. En route, it crashed in the Sierra Nevada Mountains near Bishop, CA. There were no survivors.[2]

> The President of the United States of America...takes pride in presenting the Army Distinguished Service Medal (posthumously) to Colonel Charles W. Bundy, United States Army. ... Colonel Bundy displayed superior judgment, force of character and a keen insight ... in the formulation of joint plans vital to the security of his country. Colonel Bundy was again on a mission of great importance ... when the plane in which he was a passenger crashed. He was denied by this unfortunate circumstance the rank of Brigadier General for which he had been selected.[3]

There is no way anyone could have anticipated the loss of Charles Bundy. Just a week earlier, the nation had been at peace, focused more warily upon Nazi Germany than Imperial Japan. On learning of Bundy's death, General Marshall is said to have sighed heavily, paused, and then sent for General Dwight "Ike" Eisenhower. We know the rest of the story—Ike impressed the Chief and was rapidly advanced as a result.

At first this seems a classic example of "reactive replacement," a sudden vacancy resulting in a quick grab for another officer, **any** officer—the warm body approach. Marshall's decision, however, was actually an example of thoughtful replacement planning. While the general did not know every officer in the Army personally, by late-1941 he had made a pretty thorough inventory of field grade officer talent, captured in his famous "black book" and augmented by the judgment of trusted advisors.[4] Daily wartime losses often meant selecting replacements with little deliberation, but for key senior leadership positions, Marshall refused to treat people as interchangeable parts. Having purposefully differentiated officers into talent pools in the pre-war years, he was ready to backfill the seemingly irreplaceable Bundy with the right man at the right time—Eisenhower. After years of service in the Philippines, Ike had more than Pacific theater expertise on his side. He had also gained transferrable civil and political talents that would allow him to adroitly lead a European coalition when called upon to do so.

Effective replacement planning is something that many organizations confuse with succession planning or talent management. While lying along the same continuum, each is progressively more inclusive of the total workforce:

- **Talent Management** is systematic planning for the right number and type of people to meet the organization's needs at all levels and at all times so that the majority of people are employed optimally. It integrates accessions, retention, development, and employment strategies. Talent management begins with entry-level employees and aligns their talents against the demand for them across their entire careers, to include positions at the very top of the organization.
- **Succession Planning** is a subset of talent management. It is a systematic attempt to ensure continuity of executive leadership by early cultivation of mid-career leaders through planned assessments and developmental activities. Succession planning looks much further down the talent pipeline and differentiates people into talent pools, much as we described in Chapter 5. It creates a deeper and more diverse bench of talent, increasing the odds that replacements will not be merely suitable—they will be optimal.
- **Replacement Planning** is a subset of succession planning. It manages the risk stemming from an immediate and unplanned loss of a key executive, ensuring the replacement is at least suitable to the work. Many organizations identify two or three potential replacements for each senior executive and pat themselves on the back for it. This type of limited planning usually results in replacements very much like their predecessors, regardless of the operating environment. While better than reactive replacement (which entails no planning at all), replacement planning is not enough—organi-

zations require far deeper talent pools than it engenders.

Until the Army creates an officer talent management environment running from commissioning to retirement, it cannot execute senior officer succession planning to best effect. Some near term improvements **can** be made, however, to increase the odds of getting the right officers in the right senior leadership positions. The logical start point for those improvements is a review of current practices.

CURRENT SENIOR OFFICER MANAGEMENT

What follows is a high-level look into the somewhat opaque world of senior officer management. Those managed within it are sometimes mystified by it, while those outside of it have little knowledge of how it is done.[5] Does the Army engage in thoughtful officer succession or replacement planning? Is its executive leadership engaged in and satisfied with the process?

The fact that this analysis is being written answers that last question—the last two Chiefs of Staff of the Army have identified senior officer management as an area they would like to improve. Before dissecting how it is done, however, we should acknowledge that there are factors influencing the process that are hard to control. Senate confirmation, for example, adds an element of uncertainty to general officer management. Unanticipated joint requirements present additional challenges.[6] Additionally, senior officers are not immune to illness, family pressures, job burnout, lapses in judgment, or poor performance. These things can disrupt the Army's executive succession planning, just as they do in other organizations.

The Army dedicates resources to the administrative management of senior officers. Spearheading the effort is the Senior Leader Development Office (SLD), comprised of the Colonels Management Office (COMO) and the General Officer Management Office (GOMO).[7] Prior to 2005, GOMO alone worked directly for the Army Chief of Staff, with colonel management handled by Army Human Resources Command (HRC).[8] While it routinely coordinates with HRC and Army G1, the SLD stands apart from both, residing within the Office of the Chief of Staff of the Army. Its mission is to:

> . . . assist the Chief of Staff, Army and the Secretary of the Army with the development, utilization, and management of our strategic leadership, a combined force of general officers and active duty ACC Colonels, to lead our Soldiers and civilians, and most effectively serve our Army, joint force commanders and our Nation.[9]

Within the SLD, GOMO manages approximately 415 general officers and promotable colonels (against both Army and joint requirements). The current GOMO chief explained to us the role and function of his office, which gathers and maintains administrative information, compiles personnel assessments via survey mechanisms, captures officers' preferences, and maintains candidate pools for senior officer positions. The GOMO chief meets almost weekly with both the Secretary of the Army (SECARMY) and Chief of Staff of the Army (CSA) to discuss promotions, assignments, retirements, and other management issues, and his assignment tenure is usually linked to the CSA's (approximately 4 years).

Integral to general officer management are quarterly four-star conferences, whose attendees function much like the executive management committee found in many multinational corporations. Each conference's second day is normally devoted to general officer selection, assignment, and retirement decisions. During the session, all general officer positions are discussed, and each of the four-stars recommends those they feel are best-qualified to fill pending vacancies.

Officers are assessed in accordance with several criteria. These include team fit (really "boss" fit — would their potential new boss want them?) and experience, with operational and command assignments predominating. Officer Evaluation Reports, peer reviews, and competitive selection board results are also considered. Based upon these assessments, an officer may be placed into multiple replacement pools (i.e., a three-star could be identified as a potential replacement for both the Vice Chief of Staff and the Commanding General of the Training and Doctrine Command).

Several factors heavily influence selection outcomes. Having advocates among the four-star generals is extremely important to advancing. Advocacy is often based upon the generals' first-hand experiences with those officers being considered.[10] The patronage of other key influencers also helps, such as a cabinet rank official or under secretary insisting that his or her last military advisor is "general officer material."

During the conference, GOMO's role is to recommend viable candidates for all positions, provide technical and administrative assistance, and help manage deliberations to consensus, with the Army's Chief of Staff serving as the final arbiter. The CSA then makes his recommendations to the SECARMY. When the

Secretary is satisfied with those recommendations, he nominates officers accordingly. The exception is joint three-star positions and all four-star positions—in those instances, the Secretary makes recommendations to the Secretary of Defense, who is the nominating authority.[11]

This entire process, while systematic and fairly optimal given current constraints, is much closer to replacement planning than it is to succession planning. Eliminating these constraints would engender more effective senior officer management:

Constraint #1. Senior Officer Management Falls outside the Portfolio of the Army's Chief Human Resources Officer.

As a broad body of human capital literature advises (and as several successful chief executive CEOs can attest), the Chief of HR should be the second most important person in an organization, as he or she manages its most important resource—people. Denying the Chief of HR a centerpiece role in senior officer succession planning circumscribes his or her strategic impact and signals that Army HR management is a transactional rather than transformational function. It also creates potential disconnects in a comprehensive, all-ranks officer management system. The question is, just who **is** the Army's Chief of HR? From a roles and accountabilities standpoint, the answer to that question is quite unclear.

Constraint #2. The Assignment Tenure of Key HR Leaders Does Not Align with Their Responsibilities.

We will explore this at greater length in Chapter 8, but consider that the GOMO chief, a colonel charged with the management of approximately 415 officers, typically has 4 years of assignment tenure, while the average tenure of the Army's last five G1s, charged with the management of 96,000 officers and warrant officers, 464,000 enlisted soldiers, and 331,000 DA Civilians has been about 2 years. In fact, the current CSA will likely serve with four G1s (actual or interim), all during the most significant personnel drawdown since the end of the Cold War.

Constraint #3. A Reward Culture Has Been in Operation for Decades.

Successful division commanders are almost reflexively selected for three-star positions, even if the new job is an uncertain fit with their talents. The same is true of potential division commanders. While the Army has developed brigadier generals with domain expertise in force management or public affairs, they usually do not become chiefs in those areas—those assignments appear reserved for "fast-tracking" MFE officers, future division commanders. It is not that leaders are thoughtlessly picking their protégés for jobs they may be unequal to do. They do the best they can with the talent information they have, but that information is relatively sparse.[12] As a result, they have little choice but to select a proven performer, even if that officer is a potential mismatch for the next assignment.

Constraint #4. Current and Future "Pain Points" Are Not Part of the Senior Officer Selection Equation.

In other words, senior officers are more often "chosen for the position" than "selected for the work," a failure to recognize that changes in operating environment require corresponding changes in leadership traits, experience, or expertise. A better practice would be to weigh talent supply against demand to reveal the best senior officer for each vacancy.

Talent supply considerations come down to this—is an officer being selected for current or future productivity? If it is the former, the Army should select a candidate who is ready to perform optimally, regardless of seniority. If it is the latter, the Army should select the candidate most likely to gain needed development for future employment.

Meanwhile, talent demand considerations focus upon two areas. The first is a general assessment of the work required by the position, as well as who the other members of the team are—each candidate should be assessed for job and team fit. The second area is the one most often neglected in employment considerations—the current and future situation facing the Army and the challenges that will create for the new office holder. This should have an outsized impact upon the selection process.

For example, in a May 2012 assessment, the Pentagon identified "Chinese actors" as the world's biggest perpetrators of economic espionage, noting that their ". . . attempts to collect U.S. technological and economic information will continue at a high level and will represent a growing and persistent threat to U.S. economic security." The report also noted that

China spent up to $180 billion on its military in 2011, a figure far higher than the Chinese themselves had reported.[13] This emerging threat (and all others) should significantly affect succession planning, just as other considerations should (political, economic, etc.). Can the next Army G2 or U.S. Army Cyber Command commanding general handle North Korea or Iran? Is the current G1 prepared to manage a drawdown? Will the future G8 help the Army successfully navigate uncertain fiscal waters?

With any luck, the bench of one- and two-star generals is equal to these emerging challenges. The reality, however, is that when these officers came of age in the Army, they faced different threats entirely. Some will rapidly adapt, just as Eisenhower pivoted from Pacific expert to European expert—their talents will be transferrable. Others may be less successful in confronting challenges and duties completely outside of their experience or expertise.

Constraint #5. The Army Does Not Look Far Enough Down Its Bench.

Looking further "down the bench" while continuously reassessing talent demands is what turns good replacement planning into great succession planning. General Albert C. Wedemeyer is a prime example of looking down the bench. In 1939, Captain Wedemeyer was the only active Army officer who had attended the German War College (*Kriegsakademie*). While in Berlin from 1936-38, he observed German military maneuvers firsthand, making him the Army's foremost authority on German tactical operations and strategic thought.

Promoted to major in 1940, at the outbreak of hostilities, Wedemeyer was assigned to the War Plans Division. It was there that the 41-year-old officer authored the Victory Program (War Plan "Rainbow Five"), making Germany's defeat the prime U.S. war objective despite a seemingly more immediate Japanese threat.[14] In 147 pages, Wedemeyer outlined plans for the rapid mobilization of American military and industrial power; provided remarkably accurate estimates of the materiel, organization, and equipment necessary to wage war; and laid out specific strategic guidelines for the defeat of the Axis Powers. As a result, Wedemeyer was continuously promoted over far senior officers because his talents (skill as a strategic planner, knowledge of the adversary, and dedicated, detail-oriented behavior) matched the work demanded by the times.

Does this mean that regardless of past performance, work requirements should take some proven leaders off the path to senior Army positions and open the door for others? Yes—that is the epitome of selfless service. It is only because Wedemeyer's particular talents were in demand that he advanced. In fact, had World War II been fought against the Soviets and not the Germans, perhaps Major Ivan Yeaton would have become a general instead of Wedemeyer (Yeaton was the U.S. military attaché in Moscow in the late-1930s).

The Army routinely wrestles with choosing its staff principals from the pool of two- and three-star generals—why not look further down the bench? There may be human capital, intelligence, or financial experts in the pipeline right now who could help lead the institution during a challenging era of global change, perhaps among its crop of brigadier generals or even colonels. Current management practices make selecting one of these more junior officers unlikely, of course. If there are more Wedemeyers out there, they will have to wait their turns.

Constraint #6. The Army Does not Sufficiently Differentiate Its Officers.

Because this does not occur, the senior leadership bench seems by turns too deep or too thin. GOMO reports that selecting division commanders is tough for the Army's senior leadership. There are usually several Maneuver, Fires, and Effects (MFE) candidates for each vacancy, men (and in the future, women) who are excruciatingly difficult to separate from one another because they have traveled roughly identical career paths. The Army has a surfeit of land combat experts but not enough generals' jobs for them.

Filling positions requiring nonoperational expertise is tough for a different reason — too few candidates. For example, Lieutenant General Thomas Bostick was selected from a relatively shallow pool of three candidates for Army G1 beginning those duties in February 2010. With barely a year in position, however, in April 2011, he was nominated as the Commanding General of the U.S. Army Corps of Engineers to replace Lieutenant General Robert Van Antwerp, who retired on schedule that May. In one stroke, the nomination made the G1 a lame duck and saddled him with the additional work of preparing for Senate confirmation as Chief of Engineers. It was a particularly daunting task because the preponderance of Bostick's expertise lay not in civil engineering but in combat engineering and human resource management.

No matter how talented and dedicated the general may be, turning him into a bird of passage after a year on the job had to reduce his efficacy as G1. Certainly it must have disrupted his strategic HR visioning, particularly when senators demanded his strategic Corps of Engineers vision. Just as circumstances forced Bostick to look beyond the G1, some of his HR and Army Staff teammates probably began looking beyond him—it is simply human nature.

No Army leader can be happy with this situation, one in which the Deputy Chief of Engineers wore two hats for over a year, while the sitting G1 spent countless hours preparing for a tough confirmation, one which he was ultimately able to secure. Some readers might conclude that had the Senate Armed Services Committee not delayed Bostick's confirmation as Chief of Engineers, the ripple effect upon the Army's general officer replacement plan could have been avoided. Yet it is clearly within the purview of the Senate to rigorously vet a general for near cabinet-level responsibilities, one who will lead 36,000 employees and maintain 600 dams, 926 harbors, and 12,000 miles of inland waterways. Before the Army recommends officers for a presidential nomination, it must assess the confirmation environment and make decisions accordingly. The blame cannot be leveled soley at Congress.

The larger issue is this—as we write this, the Army is over-strength in general officers, a result of diminishing joint requirements as the wars of the last decade wind down. How, then, is the talent bench so thin that one general was the only choice for two jobs? As we have said, the issue is differentiation. The Army cannot see its talent bench—other than command-centric, operational talent, it does not know what it has.

Then again, the talent bench may actually be that thin. When it comes to specialized jobs with strategic national security implications, the Army simply may not possess a sufficient supply of comptrollers, cyber warriors, civil engineers, or human capital experts. These are the types of officers who, as we discussed in Chapter 3, often hit a career ceiling as lieutenant colonels/colonels and leave the service. That leakage in the talent pipeline is a significant problem, particularly as 80 percent of senior officer assignments are nonoperational in nature—the business side of the Army.

FUTURE SENIOR OFFICER MANAGEMENT

If it sounds like we are taking the Army's leaders to task, we are not. At their direction, we are evaluating an officer personnel management system cobbled together over several generations and inherited by them—they recognize the flaws. If senior officer expertise is thin in certain areas today, it is because of decisions made years ago that failed to properly align Army human capital production with emerging requirements. Given the challenges we have described here, what can be done in the near term to improve senior officer management, to move away from "reactive" replacement and towards a more deliberate approach? We believe the Army must:

1. Manage the talents of all ranks. Junior officers are the feedstock for future generals. Managing from colonel forward is too late.

2. Create information systems capturing both individual talents and organizational talent demands.

3. Initiate individual career planning, differentiating officers into unique talent pools from 8 years of

service forward, and giving the Army a deeper bench to draw from when unanticipated challenges arise.

These changes would create an all-ranks officer talent management environment, enabling the succession planning concept shown at Figure 7-1. As officers progress through mid-career, the operations-centric management approach is left by the wayside. IDEA assessments and individual career plans differentiate officers into talent pools and cultivate their unique talents—some for employment in the operational realm (light grey), an increasing share for employment in specialized non-operational assignments (dark grey), and those few polymaths who can succeed in both worlds (hybrid).

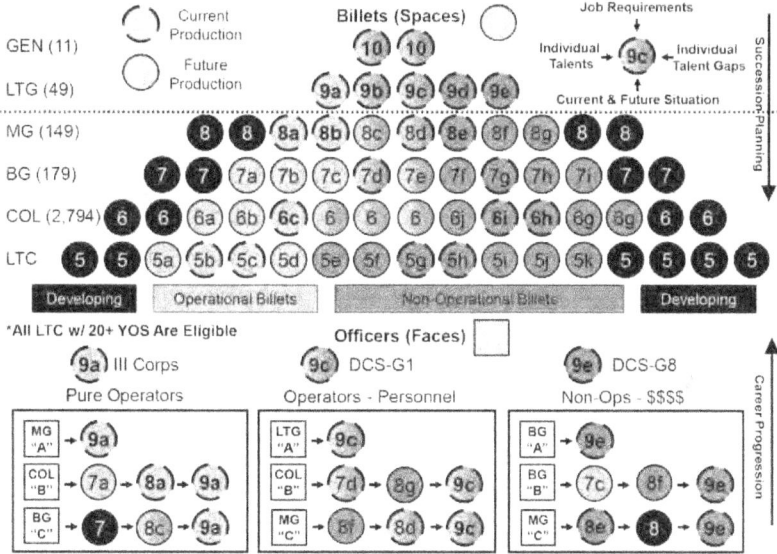

Figure 7-1. Succession and Replacement Planning Concept.

Once an officer is promoted to lieutenant colonel, his or her development should be increasingly focused within a particular expertise domain (be it land combat, acquisition, financial management, etc.). While all assignments have developmental aspects, some "non-key" jobs (in black) are designed to extend talents for future productivity while simultaneously reducing risk to the organization. Jobs requiring colonels and above are increasingly key, demanding optimal performances (current productivity). By colonel, officers should have very clearly mapped career plans, going out perhaps five years. Each officer should be aligned to one or two talent pools, with his or her strongest expertise domain having priority.

Imagine that the Senate just confirmed a new G8 (9e), and the Army wisely begins planning for both her replacement (in case of her unanticipated departure) **and** her successor (in the event she leaves the position on schedule—which means her duty assignment must have a planned duration). Looking across the bench of 149 major generals, none seems immediately suitable as a replacement. One is found (MG C), who, with perhaps two preparatory assignments, might be a good fit. MG C is therefore placed in the G8 talent pool, and his individual career plan is reviewed to ensure it prepares him accordingly. If the job becomes vacant tomorrow, he will not be ready, but if it becomes vacant in 4 years, he could be the right officer for the job. He is therefore a strong succession candidate.

Identifying just one potential successor is far too risky a proposition—several more must be found. As no other major general is a good candidate, the Army looks further down its senior officer bench. Two of 179 brigadier generals appear promising. The first candidate (BG B) has a comptroller certification and deep financial background but needs another few years of experience and development—she is also one or two assignments away from being ready. She, too, is placed into the G8 succession pool (ahead of 148 major generals), and her individual career plan will also be adjusted to prepare her for the G8 job in the future.

Still, the question of who could immediately replace the G8 in an emergency remains unanswered. The second brigadier general candidate, however (BG A), looks very promising. He thrives in complex environments, and his previous assignments, experience, and education make him a strong match for the challenges facing the G8 **today**. He thus becomes the number one replacement candidate (ahead of 148 major generals) and is a succession candidate as well. The process continues until several candidates are found to replace or succeed the G8 at different points in time (Who could do the job a year from now? Two years from now? Three years?). Just as potential G8s are identified, their replacements and successors must also be identified from within the talent pool of senior colonels, lieutenant colonels, etc.

This example demonstrates the interrelationship between replacement planning and succession planning, the crucial difference being that **succession planning looks much further down the bench**. A critical aspect of either, however, is appropriate tenure, particularly for officers in the most senior positions. As Chapter 8 will discuss, if senior officers are placed in key assignments with insufficient tenure and if those jobs are treated as rapid developmental opportunities rather than strategic leadership and management opportunities, sound replacement and succession planning become virtually impossible. The Army will find itself trapped in the world of reactive replacement—the warm body approach.

ENDNOTES - CHAPTER 7

1. Lance Berger and Dorothy Berger, eds., *The Talent Management Handbook*, New York: McGraw Hill, 2004, pp. 247-249.

2. In addition to the colonel, Major General Herbert Dargue and six other men died on the plane, which was not located until May 1942. Dargue, an Army Air Forces (AAF) officer, was the first general killed after war was declared. He was en route to Hawaii to take command of the AAF there. A veteran pilot, Dargue was likely at the controls when the B-18 went down.

3. General Orders No. 57, Washington, DC: United States War Department, 1942.

4. One was Mark Wayne Clark, who Marshall had advanced from lieutenant colonel directly to brigadier general. Clark told Marshall that Eisenhower was the only officer who could replace Bundy.

5. Our information comes from several general officer interviews, as well as discussions with the GOMO and G1 personnel.

6. An obvious example, of course, is the confirmation of General Martin Dempsey as 18th Chairman of the Joint Chiefs of Staff just months after becoming the 37th Army Chief of Staff.

7. Prior to 1973, GOMO was known as GO Branch and managed by a lieutenant colonel in the Deputy Chief of Staff for Personnel, US Army (DCSPER) (G1). In 1974, GO Branch became GOMO and migrated to the Chief of Staff of the Army's (CSA) office. By 1980, GOMO had moved back to DSCPER, where it remained until reverting back to the CSA's office in 1990.

8. The integration of COMO and GOMO within the SLD, was recognition that potential general officers must be identified and cultivated earlier in their careers. In practice, however, limited coordination between COMO and GOMO occurs. As a result, some argue that the SLD exists in name only and has not achieved its intent.

9. See Senior Leader Development website, available from *www.srleaders.army.mil/Portal2/SLD/Home.aspx.*

10. All things being equal, if more four-stars have had positive personal experience with candidate #1 than candidate #2, candidate #1 usually gets the job. In other words, it is not just "who" you know but also "how many" you know that can make the difference.

11. Donald Rumsfeld reserved division command nominations to himself, the only Secretary of Defense to do so. See Andrew Hoehn, Albert Robbert, and Margaret Harrell, *Succession Management for Senior Military Positions: The Rumsfeld Model for Secretary of Defense Involvement,* Santa Monica, CA: The Rand Corporation, 2011.

12. Recall our discussion in Chapter 4 about accounting information versus decision support information, as well as the need for a comprehensive talent information system. Compared to best corporate practices in the United States and abroad, the Army knows little about its people, even its most senior officers.

13. "China Biggest Perpetrator of Economic Spying: Pentagon," *Reuters*, May 19, 2012.

14. Wedemeyer was influential in convincing Marshall that a "Germany first" strategy was required. Marshall, in turn, prevailed upon the President to adopt that strategy.

CHAPTER 8

PROVIDE SUFFICIENT ASSIGNMENT TENURE

> Analysis of assignment tenure . . . for general officers . . . reveals . . . an illogical sequence of assignment that is impervious to external factors such as war or peace, independent of budgetary considerations, and now deeply imbedded in the institutional culture and practice. There is no valid need for this constant churning. There are, however, enormous (if unappreciated) costs associated with it.[1]
>
> Lewis Sorley

Jack Welch once said it takes 15 years for a chief executive officer (CEO) to make a difference—five to learn the job, five to produce genuine change, and five to institutionalize those changes and prepare a successor. Tenure of that length will never occur in the Army for a host of reasons. In fact, the current practice of rapid senior officer job rotation is grounded in three mutually reinforcing developments, the first of which was the 1947 Officer Personnel Act (OPA). As we explained in our preface, OPA instituted an up-or-out management system to prevent a hump of mid-career officers from blocking the advancement of younger officers.

The second is the civil-military milieu attendant to modern democracies. In the American case, it can trace its origins at least as far back as 1903, when the Army Staff system was conceived by Secretary of War Elihu Root. To placate a nervous Congress, Root's system "detailed" officers from the line to short-duration special and General Staff assignments.[2] The polite rationale was that this would keep General Staff officers connected to the field army, but the underlying reason was to preclude officers from "acquiring political and other special influence incident to long tenure" in the nation's capital.[3] In other words, the Army Staff would never become the incubator of a military aristocracy—there would be no American Ludendorff or von Hindenburg.[4]

The third is the corporate management theory and practice which held sway in the post-World War II era and heavily influenced the defense establishment. Representative of the times, in 1956, General Electric President Ralph Cordiner published a highly influential book. Titled *New Frontiers for Professional Managers*, it suggested providing executives short stints at multiple echelons across several business divisions, exposing them to as much of the company as possible. These quick moves were also viewed as a superb test of a leader's mettle. Cordiner's theories were echoed in other works and quickly became "best practice" in corporate America.

Today, however, many firms find the industrial era's rapid executive rotation model insufficient to meet the demands of a hyper-competitive Information Age economy. Even GE, which still desires some broadly experienced leaders, is increasing the job tenure of many executives, and for two reasons quite relevant to the Army:

1. To Deepen Expertise. Susan Peters, GE's Vice President of Executive Development and Chief Learning Officer, says that "The world is so complex. . . . We need people who are pretty deep." For example, GE's aircraft engine division is led by David Joyce, who has spent his entire career in GE Aviation. Previous leaders had come from outside of aviation.[5]

2. To Increase Accountability. GE realized that without allowing executives time to see a business cycle through, accountability suffered. "We were moving people every 2 years so it was musical chairs, and the joke was you could parachute into a business that was on an upswing and get all the credit," said Noel Tichy, former director of GE's Crotonville, NY, leadership center.[6]

While we are not advocating 15-year assignments for senior officers in key leadership positions, we believe that sufficient assignment tenure is critical and that it need not injure civil-military relations or clog the flow of talented officers through the ranks. Tenure, education, and succession planning are all deeply intertwined. Each has a role in ensuring the deep development of an individual's talents.

Economist and Nobel laureate Theodore Schultz argued that in every job, people are either in **equilibrium** (an ideal balance between work capabilities and work requirements) or on their way to it. When specialized education and thoughtful developmental assignments are lacking, more time on the job is required to reach equilibrium. Conversely, when domain expertise is present but time on the job is unduly brief, a senior officer cannot influence outcomes. In a study of western armies, two Australian defense analysts noted that:

> The practice of . . . rapid job rotation is one of the most idiosyncratic features of the military profession. . . . *It creates an approach to the job that is strongly focused on the short term and what can be accomplished in about a year . . .* it governs the nature, pace and scale of institutional change that is possible . . . and it has a major . . . effect on leadership styles and hence on organizational behavior, from the most senior levels down. . . .[7]

In other words, providing insufficient job tenure is like trying to win a marathon race with sprinters instead of long distance runners.

Business and organizational management theory articulates three generally accepted job phases for any newly assigned senior executive: **inquire**, **execute**, and **transition** (Welch's learn, produce, and prepare). As Figure 8-1 indicates, these readily align with both Schultz's theory of equilibrium and the Army's "mission command" concept (visualize, understand, decide, and direct). When overall job tenure is of sufficient length, appropriately selected senior officers can achieve equilibrium and perform like true locomotive engineers—controlling the bureaucratic engine's speed and direction en route to desired strategic outcomes. Without sufficient tenure, however, they are more likely to behave like locomotive firemen—stoking the engine via repetitive actions of little strategic consequence. As current Chairman of the Joint Chiefs General Martin Dempsey points out:

> We say that a leader's responsibility is to visualize, understand, decide, and direct...yet we spend the vast majority of our time providing the knowledge, skills, and attributes to allow a commander to decide and direct *and almost no time on how to visualize and understand.*[8]

Many senior officers face a terrible conundrum—if they take the time to truly visualize and understand, they have often moved on before they can decide and direct. If they move rapidly to decide and direct, their actions may create unintended consequences because they failed to appropriately visualize and understand. Increased assignment tenure helps remedy this problem, but how much tenure is sufficient to a particular senior officer job?

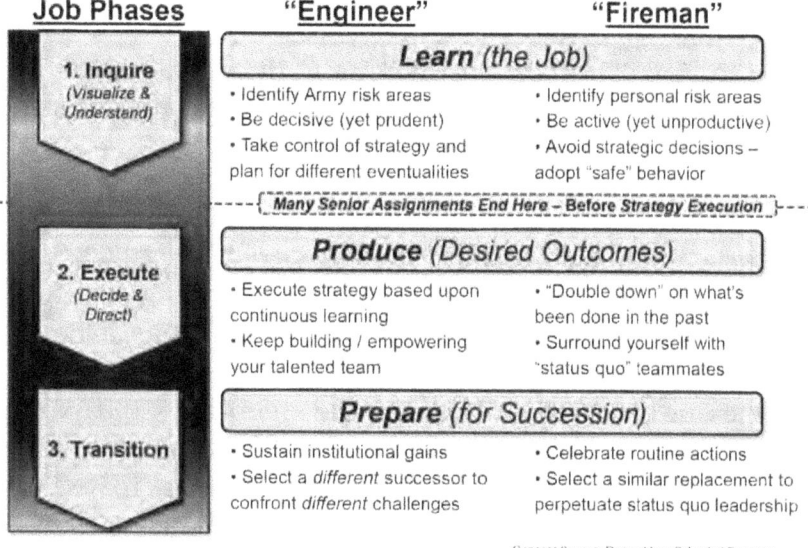

Figure 8-1. Insufficient Tenure Inhibits Strategic Outcomes.

Mutually supporting academic, corporate, and government research agrees that for truly strategic workforce assignments, 5 or more years are needed. As discussed in Chapter 5, Fortune 500 companies come close to meeting that mark, particularly among CEOs, whereas the Army experiences comparatively high senior executive churn. Beyond this, however, a range of other factors must be considered to determine the time span of discretion (tenure) required for a particular job:

1. Is the position truly strategic or key (i.e., failure would present intolerable risk)?

2. How does the assignment align with the tenure of other key leadership positions?[9]

3. Is the current occupant failing (saddling his or her successor with a lengthier than normal repair effort)?

4. Is the incoming officer a strong talent match for the work demanded (the stronger the match, the faster

the officer will arrive at equilibrium, thus shortening the "inquire" job phase)?

5. Are extraordinary changes in the operating environment complicating the work (i.e., more change management is required than in previous years)?

While all five factors are important, the last is particularly so. Consider the career of General Curtis LeMay. In 1948, LeMay became commanding general of Strategic Air Command (SAC). SAC was a new organization, one charged with maintaining a credible nuclear deterrent during the emerging Cold War with the Soviet Union. From a handful of tired B-29s and a few lackluster bomber crews, LeMay created a vaunted nuclear delivery force, one that caused many a sleepless night for the Soviet leadership. He left SAC in 1957, 9 years later. LeMay was left in command that long because the work took 9 years to do and the operating environment demanded it. No one accused the Air Force of blocking the advancement of more capable young officers because LeMay's continuous string of innovations proved he was the right man for the job.

On the subject of innovation, military historian Lewis Sorley argues that sufficient assignment tenure is critical to fostering it:

> Freed from the necessity of demonstrating their competence in a very short time, and of appearing to avoid any mistakes, [senior officers] . . . would find the environment a far more congenial and productive one, where there was room and time to *try some innovative approaches* without risking all should some not be successful.[10]

In other words, the innovations Sorely predicts (and LeMay delivered) come only when an officer has time to visualize and understand. This engenders double-loop learning, a concept first articulated by Chris Argyris and Donald Schön. Argyris, an American business theorist, posits that time for introspection improves learning and productivity. It also creates better teams. When people have time to fix mistakes, they tend to critically examine their own role in the failure. When they have no time to fix mistakes, they tend to cast blame outward. Double-loop learning is why Leonardo DaVinci, Benjamin Franklin, Marie Curie, Thomas Edison, Albert Einstein, and yes, Steve Jobs are household names. As Figure 8-2 suggests, it involves questioning underlying assumptions. It requires time for thought and experimentation. Double-loop learning is the art of asking the right questions—root cause analysis. Former Secretary of Defense Robert Gates describes it this way:

> The military will not be able to train or educate you to have all the right answers—as you might find in a manual—but you should look for those experiences and pursuits in your career that will help you at least *ask the right questions*.[11]

This ability, more than any other, allows senior officers to identify and abandon processes that consume resources without producing value. By comparison, single-loop learning takes a cursory look at the problems confronting an organization because that is all there is time for—symptoms analysis. Single-loop learning perpetuates legacy policies and practices well beyond their expiration dates.[12]

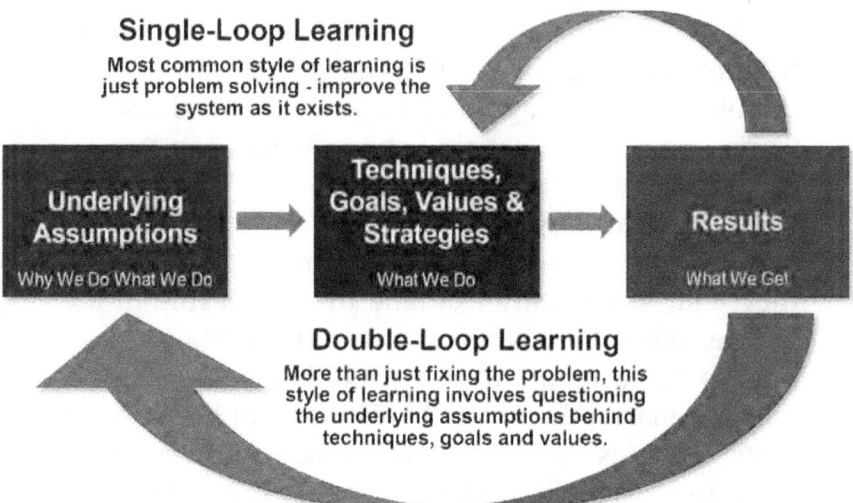

Figure 8-2. Sufficient Tenure Engenders Double-Loop Learning.[13]

There are those who argue that increased tenure, while helpful, is ultimately less beneficial than the development provided to senior officers by the rapid job rotation model. Their arguments usually echo those of GE's Cordiner and his industrial-era peers: rapid rotation engenders adaptability, it exposes the leader to more of the organization, it creates a culture of selfless service, and it maximizes the pool of broadly experienced people from which future senior officers can be drawn, maintaining the flow of talented officers into the senior officer ranks. Any such benefits are neutralized by a raft of consequences, however. In addition to the individual performance degradation we have focused upon, high churn entails higher relocation costs, undue stress upon families (particularly career-minded spouses), and reduced **team** cohesion, particularly at the strategic level.

Figure 8-3 demonstrates the impact of rapid job rotation upon teams built specifically to produce strategic outcomes—Headquarters Department of the Army (HQDA) staff sections. For example, of its 2005 complement of lieutenant colonels and above, the Office of the Chief of Staff of the Army (CSA) lost 48 percent of them the next year and an additional 24 percent the following year. In other words, every 24 months, the CSA's office experiences senior officer churn of almost 72 percent. For other staff sections, the numbers are as alarming or more so. The G3/5/7 experienced similar churn, and the Army G2 (intelligence) turned over 75 percent of its O-5s and above in 1 year. It is hard to fathom a reasonable argument for such turbulence in a wartime intelligence staff. In fact, across the Army, senior officer churn is more akin to that of fast food workers than to Fortune 500 executives.

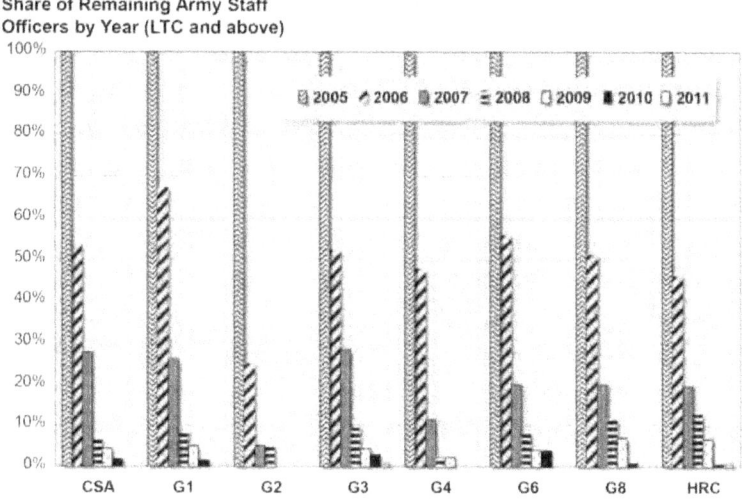

Source: U.S. Army Office of Economic and Manpower Analysis

Figure 8-3. Share of Remaining Army Staff Officers by Year (Lieutenant Colonel and Above).

Perhaps those not convinced of the perils of rapid senior officer rotation believe that the Army's civilian workforce insulates against its worst effects. Certainly, Department of the Army civilians are a terrific repository of institutional knowledge and expertise. They also serve in senior leadership positions and tend to enjoy longer job tenure than their military counterparts. But their efficacy is also undermined by the rapid loss of military supervisors and teammates. Building a cohesive civil-military staff requires assignment stability for all executives, whether civilian **or** military. Without it, civilian leaders will tend to view their military counterparts as "birds of passage" who flit into and out of the organization before making any real impact.

The last few holdouts in favor of rapid job rotation may ask, "What about maintaining the flow of officers through the ranks? Letting senior officers sit for years in one job denies those behind them the opportunities to advance or be promoted." This is the very concern that led to the creation of today's officer management system in 1947. But as discussed in Chapter 3, flow need not be a problem. As Figure 8-4 illustrates, it can be maintained through the junior ranks by normal attrition—either those who voluntarily choose to leave or who are culled from service at **Retain Point 1**. For those who stay on, at 20 years of service, a second retention decision is made (**Retain Point 2**). If an officer is not retained, he or she may retire, which also helps maintain the flow of officers through the ranks.

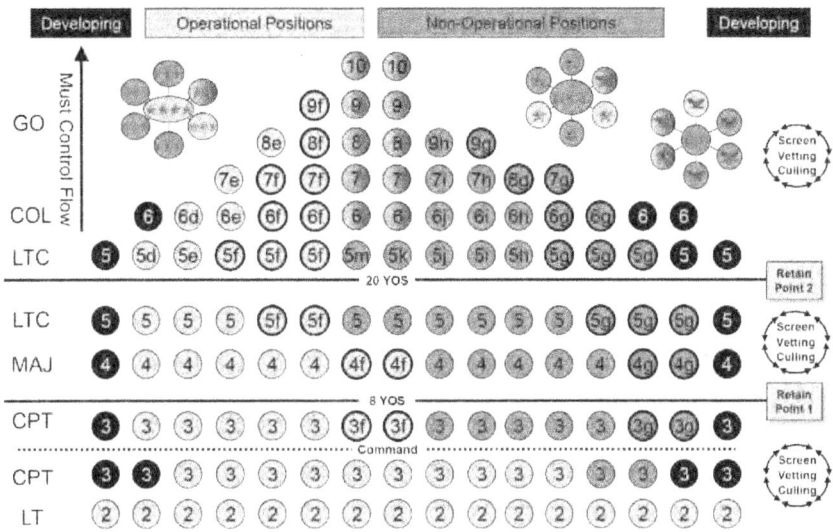

Figure 8.4. Flow of Officers Through the Ranks.

If the Army elects to retain an officer, however, he or she is immediately eligible for any and all senior officer positions based upon talent rather than grade/service. Theoretically, this means that an officer could serve as a lieutenant colonel for a year (say in position 5g), then move directly to a brigadier general's job for 3 or 4 years (7g), then move directly to a three-star position for 4 or 5 years (9g). In this example, the development lost by not rapidly rotating through colonel or major general assignments is more than offset by successful tours as a brigadier and lieutenant general, during which the officer actually had time to learn and to make a difference.[14]

If controlling the upward flow of officers really is not a problem and if the benefits of strategic tenure are as powerful as we and others have argued, why does the

Army not provide it? Perhaps it is the classic "chicken and egg" conundrum—providing senior officers with strategic tenure requires sweeping cultural and policy changes, which can only be led by senior officers with strategic tenure. That is why we are encouraged by the Army Chief of Staff's interest in this subject. As he has identified the problem early in his own tenure, his efforts to introduce officer talent management may succeed where others have not.

ENDNOTES - CHAPTER 8

1. Lewis Sorley, "The Will-o'-the-Wisp General," Paper presented at the National Conference of the Inter-University Seminar on Armed Forces and Society, Chicago, IL, October 25, 1980, p. 2.

2. Root did all he could to ameliorate congressional concerns regarding the creation of a general staff for a standing (albeit tiny) army. As he said:

> Neither our political nor our military system makes it suitable that we should have a general staff organized like the German general staff . . .; but the common experience of mankind is that the things which those general staffs do . . . have to be done by a body of men especially assigned to do them. . . . It is not an executive body . . . it acts only through the authority of others.

See Thomas Harry Williams, *Americans at War: The Development of the American Military System*, Baton Rouge, LA: Louisiana State University Press, 1960, p. 102.

3. Otto L. Nelson, Jr., "National Security and the General Staff," Washington, DC: Infantry Journal Press, 1946, p. 14.

4. Resistance came from inside the Army as well. Lieutenant General Nelson Miles, the Army's commanding general, lambasted Root's reforms for seeming to "Germanize . . . the small Army of the United States." Washington, DC: U.S. Senate 1902, p. 34.

5. Kate Linebaugh, "The New GE Way: Go Deep, Not Wide," *The Wall Street Journal*, March 7, 2012.

6. *Ibid.*

7. Nicholas Jans and Judy Frazier-Jans, "Career Development, Job Rotation and Professional Performance," *Armed Forces and Society Magazine*, Winter 2004, pp. 255-256. Italics are ours.

8. Thomas Friedman and Michael Mandelbaum, *That Used to Be Us*, New York: Farrar, Straus and Giroux, 2011, pp. 88-89. Italics are ours.

9. For example, at the time we wrote this, the average assignment tenure of the Army's four-star generals (excluding the Chairman of the Joint Chiefs of Staff) was just over 15 months. One (at Army Materiel Command) had been in command for 42 months. Without that general, the average tenure dropped below 12 months. This was because seven of nine Army four-star positions changed leadership in a 14-month span. While each four-star may serve a fairly lengthy time in position, it is indicative of another critical succession planning consideration—replacement **timing** across collaborating staffs and organizations.

10. Sorley, p. 22. Italics are ours.

11. Secretary of Defense Robert Gates, Speech at West Point, NY, February 25, 2011, available from *www.defense.gov/speeches/speech.aspx?speechid=1539*.

12. Colonel (later Major General) George Crook is a good example of a double-loop learner. A Civil War veteran, by 1871, he was leading the Army's Arizona Department against the Chiricahua Apaches, among the best foot soldiers the world has ever seen. His predecessors had failed to pacify the Apaches, in part because they relied upon horses and wagons for transport and supply—standard Army practice. Crook instead used mule trains to pursue the Apaches across terrain that wagons could not negotiate, denying his adversaries a safe haven from which to operate—double-loop learning.

13. Source: *Leadership Now*, "Leading Blog," May 13, 2008, available from *www.leadershipnow.com/leadingblog/2008/05/learning_requires_personal_res.html*.

14. On the subject of commissioned rank, in our view, it serves three purposes: (1) To provide authorities consistent with an officer's duties and responsibilities, (2) to signal that authority to others, and (3) to signal the productive outcomes that the officer can deliver. The higher the rank associated with a duty position, the more strategic it should be. In turn, the more strategic a position is, the greater its assignment tenure should be, so that strategic outcomes can actually be delivered. Because the Army associates rank with an individual's time in service rather than with duty demands, its senior officer structure is significantly overbuilt (the same holds true in the other services). As a result, lieutenant generals supervise major generals, who in turn supervise brigadier generals, who in turn supervise colonels, all of whom rotate so rapidly from assignment to assignment that such supervision is often superfluous and ineffectual. High churn reinforces hierarchical models. Lower churn would allow for flatter, more collaborative work structures, something discussed in a follow-on paper.

CHAPTER 9

PREPARE FOR CHANGE

> Perhaps the greatest difficulty . . . in preparing future leaders has to do with a personnel system that derives its philosophical and instrumental basis from reforms conducted between 1899 and 1904. . . . The current system has its roots in long outdated mobilization systems for mass armies in world wars. . . . That state of affairs must change.
>
> 2010 Joint Operating Environment[1]

To this point, we have recommended senior officer management practices grounded in human capital theory, data, and analysis, practices which have proven beneficial in government and private sector organizations alike. Rather than focusing narrowly upon colonels and above, we have placed our proposals within a larger officer corps context because they must be. Junior officers are the feedstock for senior officers in a limited lateral entry labor market—the former must be carefully managed to produce the latter.

Comprehensive officer talent management requires more than the recommendations we have made here, however. It also needs a phased implementation plan, with clearly articulated roles, responsibilities, and success measures. Any changes in policy and practice will require piloting, and **all** changes must be made in truly integrative fashion.

We believe such an approach must be preceded by two things, however. The first is culture change, an acknowledgment that talent management is not just a "human resources (HR) thing"—it is something an entire organization undertakes to reach desired outcomes. Talent management must become part of the Army's DNA. The second is a deep redesign of Army HR, moving from a transactional HR system to a transformational one. Management consultant Dorothy Berger describes that type of organization in this way:

> The primary responsibility for future human resource professionals will become talent management. . . . To become better positioned to manage talent and maximize performance . . . [they] will shed transactional work activities. Much of the present human resource function will be outsourced, made directly available to employees through the use of technology, or delegated to line managers. The focus for human resource practitioners will be on creating a work culture that nurtures talent by offering customized employment packages, providing the empowerment and freedom needed by skilled workers, and instilling a cohesive, supportive culture into diverse workforces.[2]

Nothing is more important than raising the productivity and intellectual capital of an organization, and an HR system like the one Berger describes is the best way to do it. Yet in companies and organizations across America, this type of HR remains the exception rather than the rule. HR remains the enterprise function people love to hate. Millions of Americans have experienced the tender ministrations of administratively focused HR departments. These departments treat people like lines on a balance sheet, using verbs such as "procure, distribute, account, collect, process, store"[3] instead of "assess, evaluate, counsel, support, advise, represent."

Why? In part, it is due to an outsized focus upon supposed fairness, to prevent companies from running afoul of a dense thicket of policies and regulations. After all, will treating people uniquely open an organization to charges of bias? The other reason is that it is simply easier to measure what is done than what is delivered, to pursue short-term cost efficiency instead of long-term value. Just like thousands of American HR departments, Army HR focuses upon standardization and uniformity in the face of a workforce that is heterogeneous and complex. It pursues what is organizationally expedient at the expense of increased productivity and satisfaction.

Senior officers are increasingly aware of this and desire change. In fact, a 2011 survey found that 65 percent of active duty generals rated "personnel management" as one of the worst performing functions in the Army. As one noted, "Human capital is the most important yet the least agile system. . . . As an Army of people, the thing we do worst is managing those people."[4] Army HR challenges map to the sectors depicted in Figure 9-1, which will be discussed in turn.

Figure 9-1. Human Resource Challenges.[5]

- **Profession.** As we touched upon in Chapter 4, today's Army HR system is inordinately process driven, its strategic role circumscribed by both policy and practice. Army HR professionals are trapped in an outmoded design. Furthermore, while its transactional wing (HRC) is manned by great civilians, officers, and soldiers, they are rarely HR professionals in the conventional sense. Many are infantrymen, aviators, artillerists, and signal officers, all pressed into service by their branches for a tour at Fort Knox, KY, each often rotating through two or three jobs during their assignment. For the most part, not even the Adjutant General officers and Soldiers in the command (or in the Army HR community-at-large) are credentialed human capital experts.

  As a result, while the Army is somewhat adept in the administrative art of personnel management, today it lacks the expertise to deliver talent management, the **science** of extracting greater productivity at lower cost from more satisfied employees. Talent management, enabled by sound theory, data, and analysis, is rapidly increasing the effectiveness, competitiveness, and intellectual capital of organizations enlightened enough to do it. The Army should become as enlightened. Creating professional HR organizations with a greater share of human capital domain expertise is a critical step to getting there.

- **Influence.** Why do 65 percent of Army generals think that HR is such a poorly performing function? How can this be explained, particularly as their high performing peers are continuously working in the HR realm? The answer is found in our previous chapters: lack of authority, domain expertise, or tenure (and thus, lack of accountability).

In top-flight HR systems, the Chief of Human Resources is often the long-serving number two person in the organization, a true HR expert. Meanwhile, the Army G1 is not number two, number five, or even number 10. He has much less authority than many of his civilian counterparts. For example, the G1 has little role in senior officer replacement or succession planning, a critical HR function. He also lacks routine access to the Chief of Staff or Secretary of the Army. Finally, he is usually a combat arms officer with very little of the time (or expertise) needed to effect change.

Of course, the Army G1 does not really lead Army HR, which is a strategically challenged grouping of disparate organizations, ostensibly coordinating within the "Human Capital Enterprise" (HCE).[6] The HCE is headed by the Assistant Secretary of the Army for Manpower and Reserve Affairs (ASA/M&RA) and the Commanding General of TRADOC, whose responsibilities and day-to-day activities are so extensive that HR collaboration between them is a challenge, one exacerbated by geography (the M&RA and G1 are in the Pentagon, Washington, DC; TRADOC is at Fort Eustis, VA; and Army Human Resources Command is at Fort Knox, KY).

In short, senior Army HR leaders preside over transactional rather than transformational activities because policy, tradition, and poor organizational design deny them the expertise, authority, and tenure needed to wield genuine influence. This must change. As the Army's HR domain is increasingly manned with tenured HR professionals, they must demand a seat at the table, fearlessly offering their expertise to transform Army HR from a process-oriented, current-focused domain into a people-oriented, future-focused one. This will allow them to lead the development of innovative HR practices rather than continuing to staff actions in accordance with decades-old policies.

- **Skills.** There is an obvious connection between the skills and professionalism of any HR system. As we discussed in Chapter 4, today's Army HR (particularly HRC) possesses important skills, particularly in the Administrative Expert role. It also possesses some strength as an Employee Relations Expert but is less influential as a Strategic Partner or Change Agent. To improve in those areas, Army HR needs to augment its existing skills. Moving beyond routine transactional activities, it must also design and undertake transformational ones. This requires professionals with education and expertise in areas such as behavioral economics, career counseling, consultation and performance improvement, etc. These certified experts will be true talent masters. Expert in **performance management** rather than **requirements management**, they will understand that taking care of the former is the best way to satisfy the latter.

- **Perception.** Despite their hard work, Army HR people know that they are often perceived as organizational enforcers rather than employee advocates. There is an opaqueness to current Army HR processes (particularly assignments), which many officers find off-putting, particularly at the junior and mid-career ranks. Genuine performance management should go a long way towards changing their perceptions of Army HR, however. This is critical because today's enormously competitive labor market gives educated professionals the option of seeking new employment whenever a company fails to give them sufficient voice in their work. The industrial era, during which "bosses" unilaterally made employment decisions, is over. Current and future generations need not, and **will** not, accept opaque human resource practices. People want greater voice in their careers. If the Army does not give it to them, someone else will.

Summing up, the table-setting changes we are suggesting in this chapter are:

1. Commit to an evolution from one-size-fits-all, time-based personnel management to individually tailored, productivity-focused talent management. Ruthlessly enforce change across the Army — talent management transcends the HR domain.

2. Identify an unambiguous chief of all Army HR systems and processes (with ASA/M&RA retaining oversight).

3. Identify and appoint tenured HR transformation leaders in the following key billets: Army G1 (5 years), Army G1/Director of Military Personnel Management (4 years), Army G1/SIG (3 years), Commanding General, HRC (4 years), and HRC/Chief, Officer Personnel Management Directorate (4 years). Review and identify other key HR domain billets and provide sufficient tenure for each.

4. Make human capital management education and expertise the centerpiece criteria in the selection and appointment of officers throughout the Army HR domain.

5. Move from a transactional HR system to a transformational one. Create an internal HR consultancy focused more upon people and less upon process.

If the Army makes a true commitment to culture change, if it revises its HR vision as described here, it will be postured to introduce the genuine officer talent management policies we conclude with in our next and final chapter. Those policies will not only create a far more adaptable senior officer cohort—they will create virtuous effects cascading across all officer ranks.

ENDNOTES - CHAPTER 9

1. *Joint Operating Environment 2010*, Norfolk, VA: U.S. Joint Forces Command, 2010, p. 71.

2. Lance Berger and Dorothy Berger, eds., *The Talent Management Handbook*, New York: McGraw Hill, 2004, p. 39.

3. These are from *Pamphlet 600-3*, Washington, DC: Department of the Army, February 2010, p. 353, articulating the Adjutant General Corps' officer core competencies.

4. Secretary of the Army's AUSA Annual Meeting opening ceremony remarks, October 10, 2011, available from *www.army.mil/article/67109/Oct__10__2011____Secretary_of_the_Army_s_AUSA_Annual_Meeting_opening_ceremony_remarks/*.

5. See Richard M. Vosburgh, "The Evolution of HR: Developing HR as an Internal Consulting Organization," *Human Resources Planning and Strategy*, Vol. 30, No. 3, September 2007, available from *www.hrps.org/resource/resmgr/p_s_article_preview/hrps_issue30.3_evolutionofhr.pdf*.

6. Ask 10 Army professionals (officer, enlisted, or civilian) who leads Army HR. Our guess is that you will get at least three different answers.

CHAPTER 10

CONCLUSIONS — THE WAY AHEAD

> If we don't get the people right, the rest of it won't matter. We're going to put the country at risk.[1]
>
> General Martin Dempsey

We have argued that many senior officer management challenges are achingly old, representing years of accumulated practices that have outlived their effectiveness. To support that argument, we relied not only upon our own analysis, but also upon the mutually reinforcing findings of academic, government, Department of Defense (DoD), and Army studies spanning several decades. One of the most powerful and oft-repeated concerns emerging from our study review is that senior Army officers seem unable to lead rapid institutional adaptation in a world that increasingly demands it.

No one is more concerned by this challenge than today's Army leaders, who asked us to examine current senior officer management practices and suggest necessary improvements. As we did so, however, it immediately became clear that any improvements to senior officer management must be firmly rooted within a comprehensive, Army-wide evolution towards all-ranks officer **talent** management, one that provides both the structural and career flexibility needed to respond to whatever unanticipated crises the future may bring.

In Chapter 3, we articulated a foundational talent management framework for the entire officer corps, one grounded in sound human capital theory. That theory holds that all officers possess varied and unique talent distributions, just as all officer requirements are varied and unique. The nexus of that talent supply and demand must be carefully managed across the interrelated activities of the Officer Human Capital Model—accessions, retention, development, and employment, supported by continuous evaluation mechanisms.

Doing so, however, requires talent information that the Army does not yet have. As a result, it has little choice but to take a one-size-fits-all approach to officer management, one heavily focused upon creating land combat expertise. This approach, while well-suited to producing junior officers, is less effective at producing senior officers, whose assignments become increasingly nonoperational as they advance in rank. As a result, talent mismatches often occur, with superb senior leaders being placed in assignments for which the Army has failed to prepare them—the highly specialized and complex business side of the Army.

To remedy this, we propose two innovations: eliminating year group management at the 8th year of service and implementing comprehensive officer assessments (IDEAs) at key crossroads in each officer's career. These initiatives will provide an overarching officer talent management framework, one that creates a stable balance between officer requirements and inventory. Once this framework is established, additional talent management initiatives can be implemented across five change imperative areas. As outlined in Chapter 2, they are:

1. Differentiate people—seek and employ a diverse range of talents.
2. Develop relevant and specialized expertise via individual career paths.
3. Invest in higher and specialized education.
4. Improve succession planning.
5. Provide sufficient assignment tenure.

Officer Human Capital Policy—Desired Outcomes and Recommendations.

We will use the change imperatives to summarize the recommendations we have made throughout the monograph. With thoughtful piloting and implementation, we believe these imperatives will create a more adaptable senior officer cohort and Army, with virtuous effects cascading across all officer ranks. While our recommendations are not all inclusive, we strongly suggest that they form the basis of a comprehensive HR system overhaul, one grounded within the talent management framework presented. That overhaul is long overdue because the current HR system was arrived at incrementally, in response to labor market conditions and challenges that, for the most part, no longer exist.

If our recommendations are implemented, we believe they will yield an all-ranks officer talent management system that realizes the following desired outcomes:

A. Aligns Professional Military Education (PME) with Individual Development and Employment Assessments (IDEAs).

B. Increases PME rigor to enhance its efficacy as a screening, vetting, and culling tool.

C. Uses PME to certify each officer's expertise for entry into the next career phase.

D. Promotes individual career paths, deep succession planning, and appropriate tenure.

As Figure 10-1 shows, this will provide a pathway to senior leadership that better aligns human capital production with requirements across the Officer Career Model. In other words, the Army's supply of officer talent will better match the demand for it at all echelons, from commissioning to the highest levels of leadership.

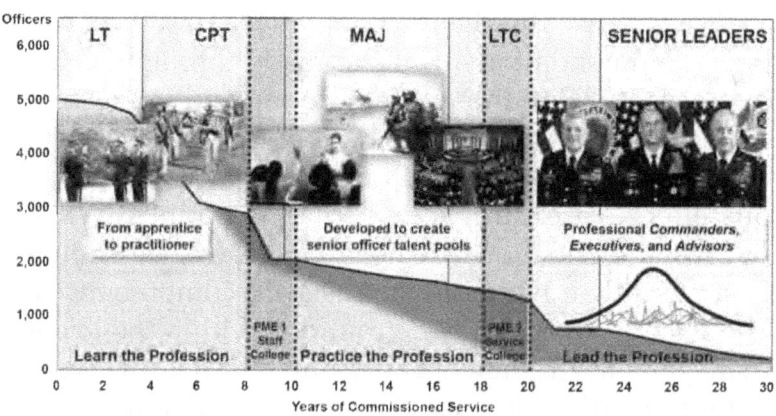

Figure 10-1. Desired Outcomes.

The five change imperatives provide a conceptual roadmap to achieving these outcomes. For each, specific action items to undergird implementation are identified. They are:

1. Differentiate people—seek and employ a diverse range of talents.

   a. Implement use of a talent management information system across the entire officer corps (to include at the commissioning sources).

   b. Provide a dedicated career counselor and mentor to each officer.

c. Differentiate people into domain expertise talent pools via IDEAs at key career crossroads. Align IDEAs with professional military education attendance whenever possible.

d. Implement use of the nine-box talent matrix during IDEA assessments.

e. Use IDEA assessments to cull officers lacking the requisite talents for service in the Army profession.

f. Pilot the IDEA assessment process to refine an implementation plan.

2. Develop relevant and specialized expertise via individual career paths.

a. Use IDEA assessments to periodically collect granular information on each officer's **performance, potential, readiness,** and **suitability** for service in particular branches or functional areas.

b. Based upon IDEA assessments, create individual career plans for each officer. Beginning at the 8th year of service, manage officers by talents rather than by year group.

c. Expand the pathways to senior Army leadership, allowing business and management expertise to complement (not replace) operational acumen. Align the production of domain expertise with the demand for it.

d. Identify **key** billets among all O-6 and above positions across the Army. **Key** = requires current productivity (the officer is "in equilibrium") — failure incurs unacceptable risk.

e. Use nonkey billets to provide low-risk developmental opportunities.

f. Consider team fit when making officer assignments.

3. Invest in higher and specialized education.

a. Make resident advanced civil schooling mandatory for all senior officers.

b. Adjust the officer Trainees, Transients, Holdees, and Students (TTHS) accordingly to accommodate a higher proportion of advanced civil schooling students at any particular moment.

c. Decrease reliance upon senior service colleges to provide master's degrees. Use them instead as corporate universities, complementing senior officer advanced civil schooling with joint and strategic land combat education.

d. Increase academic rigor at the staff and service colleges, which provide an ideal opportunity to conduct penetrating talent assessments of each officer — once (ILE) as they prepare for mid-career as field grade officers, and again (War College) as they prepare to transition to the senior officer ranks.

e. Provide specialized, domain-specific continuing education to senior officers.

4. Improve succession planning.

a. Integrate senior officer replacement and succession planning within an all ranks officer talent management system. Implement this planning as soon as talent information (on both the supply and demand sides) makes it possible.

b. Look as far down the leadership bench as necessary to find the right person for the job — make talent-based rather than seniority-based assignment decisions.

    c. Consider current and future "pain points" when selecting officers for key positions—are they suited to the particular demands they will face, which will differ from those of their predecessor?
    d. Heavily weight functional expertise and education when selecting officers for nonoperational assignments (HR, finances, public affairs, etc.).

 5. Provide sufficient assignment tenure.
    a. Recognize that the more strategic an officer's responsibilities, the longer must be her/his assignment tenure.
    b. Use increased assignment tenure to deepen expertise and increase accountability.
    c. Reduce officer churn in Army organizations expected to achieve strategic outcomes.
    d. Consciously align the tenure of officers with teammates to protect against loss of institutional knowledge.

In closing, let us be clear. If we valued "domain expertise" above all else, we would suggest populating the entire institutional Army with civilians. We are not arguing for business or administrative expertise at the expense of soldiering—we are arguing for both. The Army is a land combat profession. As currently serving and retired officers, we believe it should be led by men and women who apprentice in operational assignments but are prepared to successfully **lead change** at the echelon-above-corps and institutional level. Full career, all-ranks officer talent management is the best way to prepare them. Talent management is a proven, inherently American innovation that dramatically enhances productivity and employee satisfaction. Adopting it is not a question of "corporate practice" versus military culture. It is good practice, period.

ENDNOTE - CHAPTER 10

1. Andrew Lapin, "Dempsey Maps Sequestration Cuts at Defense," *Government Executive*, June 19, 2012, available from *www.govexec.com/defense/2012/06/dempsey-maps-sequestration-cuts-defense/56353/%3Foref%3Dtop-story*.

BIBLIOGRAPHY

Allen, Charles D. "Redress of Professional Military Education: The Clarion Call." *Joint Force Quarterly*, Issue 59, 4th Quarter 2010.

Arabian, Jane M. and Jennifer A. Shelby. "Policies, Procedures, and People: The Initial Selection of U.S. Military Officers." *Officer Selection*, Nueilly-Sur-Seine Cedex, France: NATO Research and Technology Organization, 2000.

Army Field Manual 6-22, Army Leadership: Competent, Confident and Agile. Washington, DC: Department of the Army, October 12, 2006.

Army Pamphlet 600-3, Commissioned Officer Professional Development and Career Management. Washington, DC: Department of the Army, February 1, 2010.

Army Pamphlet 600-65. Leadership Quotes. Washington, DC: Department of the Army, November 1985.

Army Regulation 600-8-29, Officer Promotions. Washington, DC: Department of the Army, February 25, 2005.

Army Regulation 621-108, Military Personnel Requirements for Civilian Education. Washington, DC: Department of the Army, March 26, 2007.

Armstrong, Thomas. *7 Kinds of Smart: Identifying and Developing Your Multiple Intelligences*. New York: Penguin Group, 1999.

Arnold, Isaac N. *The Life of Abraham Lincoln*, 4th Ed. New York: Bison Books, 1994.

Baldwin, Hanson W. "The Problem of Army Morale." *New York Times Magazine*, December 5, 1954.

_____. "What's Wrong with the Regulars," *Saturday Evening Post*, October 31, 1953.

Bautz, Edward, Jr. "Imponderables of Officer Personnel Management." Student Thesis, Carlisle, PA: U.S. Army War College, March 19, 1958.

Becker, Gary. *Human Capital*, 3rd Ed. Chicago, IL: University of Chicago Press, 1993.

Berger, Lance and Dorothy Berger, eds. *The Talent Management Handbook*. New York: McGraw Hill, 2004.

Blumenson, Martin. "America's World War II Leaders in Europe: Some Thoughts." *Parameters*, December 1989.

Bowles, Samuel, Herbert Gintis, and Melissa Osborne. "The Determinants of Earnings: A Behavioral Approach." *Journal of Economic Literature*, Vol. 39, No. 4, December 2001.

Burk, James. "Military Mobilization in Modern Western Societies," in Guiseppe Carforio, ed., *Handbook of the Sociology of the Military*. New York: Kluwer Academic/Plenum Publishers, 2003.

Cappelli, Peter. *Talent on Demand*. Boston, MA: Harvard Business Press, 2008.

Chairman of the Joint Chiefs of Staff Instruction 1331.01D: "Manpower and Personnel Actions Involving General and Flag Officers," August 1, 2010.

Chairman of the Joint Chiefs of Staff Instruction 1800.01D: "Officer Professional Military Education Policy," July 15, 2009.

"China Biggest Perpetrator of Economic Spying: Pentagon." *Reuters*, May 19, 2012.

Clarke, Richard. "China's Cyberassault on America." *The Wall Street Journal*, June 15, 2011.

Coffman, Edward M. *The Regulars: The American Army, 1898-1941*. Cambridge, MA: Belknap Press of Harvard University Press, 2004.

Coffman, Edward M. and Peter F. Herrly. "The American Regular Army Officer Corps Between the World Wars: A Collective Biography." *Armed Forces and Society*, Vol. 4, November 1, 1977.

Colby, Elbridge. *The Profession of Arms*. New York and London, UK: D. Appleton and Company, 1924.

College Board, *Trends in College Pricing*, Washington, DC, 2007.

Conaty, Bill and Ram Charan. *The Talent Masters*. New York: Crown Business Press, 2010.

Congressional Research Service, "Army Officer Shortages: Background and Issues for Congress," Washington, DC, July 5, 2006.

Corona, Victor P. "Career Patterns in the U.S. Army Officer Corps." New York: Center on Organizational Innovation, Columbia University, April 6, 2010.

Corporate Leadership Council. "Succession Planning in the Government Sector," January 2004.

Coumbe, Arthur T. and Lee S. Harford. *U.S. Army Cadet Command: The 10 Year History.* Washington, DC: Government Printing Office, 1996.

Coumbe, Arthur T. and Paul Kotakis. *History of U.S. Army Cadet Command: The Second Ten Years, 1996-2006.* Washington, DC: U.S. Government Printing Office, 2008.

Davies, Anna *et al.* "Future Work Skills 2020" Institute for the Future, Phoenix, AZ: University of Phoenix Research Institute, 2011.

Deans, Graeme and Kathy Kalafatides. "Leader-Sheep: Lessons Learned from the Crisis." *Ivey Business Journal*, September/October 2010.

Defense Science Board. "Enhancing Adaptability of U.S. Military Forces, Part A. Main Report." Washington, DC: Office of the Under Secretary of Defense for Acquisition, Technology and Logistics, January 2011.

De Fruyt, Filip and Ivan Mervielde. "RIASEC Types and Big Five Traits as Predictors of Employment Status and Nature of Employment." *Personnel Psychology*, Vol. 52, 1999.

Dempsey, Martin E. "Leader Development." *Army Magazine*, February, 2011.

_____. "Win, Learn, Focus, Adapt, Win Again." Washington, DC: Institute of Land Warfare, Association of the United States Army, March, 2011.

D'Este, Carlo. *Eisenhower: A Soldier's Life*. New York: Henry Holt and Co., 2002.

Dixon, Norman F. *On the Psychology of Military Incompetence*. New York: Basic Books, Inc., 1976.

Driscoll, Molly and Jamie Matthews-Mead. "Taking Charge of Your Professional and Career Development." Columbus, OH: Ohio State University, March, 2011.

Dupuy, R. Ernest. "Pass in Review," *The Army Combat Forces Journal*, Vol. 5, No. 3, October 1954.

"Extraordinary Commitment: Challenges and Achievements of Today's Working Learner." *University of Phoenix Working Learner Spotlights*, September, 2010.

Freedman, Anne. "Master of HR at GE." *Human Resource Executive Online*. October 16, 2004, available from www.hreonline.com/HRE/story.jsp?storyId=4222837.

Freytag-Loringhoven, Hugo. "The Power of Personality in War." *The Roots of Strategy*, Vol. 3. Mechanicsville, PA: Stackpole Books, 1991.

Friedman, Thomas and Michael Mandelbaum. *That Used to Be Us*. New York: Farrar, Straus, and Giroux, 2011.

Gardner, Howard. "Multiple Intelligences after Twenty Years." Paper presented at the American Educational Research Association, Chicago, IL, April 21, 2003.

_____. *Frames of Mind: The Theory of Multiple Intelligences*, 20th Anniversary Ed. New York: Basic Books, 2004.

Gates, Robert M. "Speech at West Point Banquet." West Point, NY, February 25, 2011. U.S. Department of Defense, available from *www.defense.gov/Speeches/Speech.aspx?SpeechID=1539*.

Generation Y: "The Millennials—Ready or Not, Here They Come." Information Paper, Cleveland, OH: NAS Recruitment Communications, 2006.

Ginsburgh, Robert N. "The Challenge to Military Professionalism," *Foreign Affairs*, January 1964.

Gittell, Jody Hoffer. "Relational Coordination: Guidelines for Theory, Measurement and Analysis." The Heller School for Social Policy and Management, Waltham, MA: Brandeis University, January, 2009.

_____. *The Southwest Airlines Way*. New York: McGraw-Hill, 2003.

Gladwell, Malcolm. "Late Bloomers." *The New Yorker*, October 20, 2008.

Government Accountability Office. Exposure Draft, *A Model of Strategic Human Capital Management*, GAO-02-373SP, Washington, DC: U.S. Government Accountability Office, March, 2002.

Gubman, Edward L. *The Talent Solution*, New York: McGraw-Hill, 1998.

Hall, Douglas T. *Careers In and Out of Organizations*. Thousand Oaks, CA: Sage Publications, Inc., 2002.

Hall, Pippa. "Interprofessional Teamwork: Professional Cultures as Barriers." *Journal of Interprofessional Care*, Supplement 1, May 2005.

Ham, Carter F., Commanding General, AFRICOM, *Interview with Authors*. West Point, NY, October 2011.

Hargrove, Robert. "Master Mentor 3: Fox Connor, The Man Who Made Ike," April 8, 2008, available from *www.roberthargrove.com/master-mentor-3-fox-connor-the-man-who-made-ike/*.

Harrell, Margaret *et al*. "A Future Officer Career Management System: An Objectives-Based Design." Santa Monica, CA: RAND National Defense Research Institute, 2001.

_____. "General and Flag Officer Careers: Consequences of Increased Tenure." Santa Monica, CA: RAND National Defense Research Institute, 2001.

Haught, David D. "Officer Personnel Management in the Army: Past, Present, and Future," Carlisle, PA: U.S. Army War College, April 7, 2003.

Headquarters, Department of the Army. "General Orders No. 7, Establishment of the United States Army Human Resources Command (HRC)." Washington, DC, September 30, 2003.

Heifetz, Ronald A. *Leadership Without Easy Answers*. Cambridge, MA: Harvard University Press, 1994.

Hernandez, Rhett. Commanding General, U.S. Army Cyber Command, interview with authors, West Point, NY, October 28, 2011.

Herron, Charles D. "Efficiency Reports." *The Infantry Journal*, Vol. LIV, April 1944.

Hill, David C. "Junior Officer Institutional Leadership Education: Is the Basic Officer Leadership Course (BOLC) Meeting the Challenge?" Carlisle, PA: U.S. Army War College, July 1, 2008.

Hodges, H. Charles. "The United States Army War College: Time for a Change." U.S. Army War College Strategy Research Project. Carlisle, PA: U.S. Army War College, March 23, 2012.

Hughes, Daniel J. "Professors in the Colonels' World." *Military Culture and Education*, Douglas Hightree, ed., London, UK: Ashgate Publishing, 2011.

Huntington, Samuel P. "Power, Expertise, and the Military Profession." *Daedalus*, Fall 1963.

Iverson, George R. "Officer Personnel Management: A Historical Perspective." Study Project, Carlisle PA: US Army War College, May 12, 1978.

Janowitz, Morris. *The Professional Soldier*. London, UK: Times Publishing Company, Ltd., 1962.

Jans, Nicholas. "The 'Once Were Warriors' Syndrome and Strategic Leadership in the Profession of Arms." *CDCLMS Leadership Papers*, March 2004.

Jans, Nicholas and Judy Frazier-Jans. "Career Development, Job Rotation and Professional Performance." *Armed Forces and Society Magazine*, Winter 2004.

Johnson, David E. "Preparing Potential Senior Army Leaders for the Future: An Assessment of Leader Development Efforts in the Post-Cold War Era." Santa Monica, CA: Rand Arroyo Center, 2002.

Johnson, Harold K. "The Army's Role in Nation Building and Preserving Stability." *Army Information Digest*, November, 1965.

Johnson-Freese, Joan. "Teach Tough, Think Tough: Why Military Education Must Change." *AOL Defense*, June 15, 2011, available from *defense.aol.com/2011/06/15/teach-tough-think-tough/*.

Kamphausen, Roy, Andrew Scobell, and Travis Tanner, eds. *The 'People' in the PLA: Recruitment, Training, and Education in China's Military*. Carlisle, PA: Strategic Studies Institute, U.S. Army War College, September 2008.

Kaplan, Steven N. *et al*. "Which CEO Characteristics and Abilities Matter?" Cambridge, MA: National Bureau of Economic Research Working Paper No. 14195, July 2008.

Kesler, Gregory C. "Why the Leadership Bench Never Gets Deeper: Ten Insights About Executive Talent Development." *HR Planning Society Journal*, Vol. 25, No. 1, 2002.

Knudson, Leslie. "Generating Leaders GE Style." *HR Management Online*.

Kozak, Warren. *Lemay: The Life and Wars of General Curtis LeMay*. New York: Regnery Publishing, Inc., 2009.

Kydland, F. E. and E. C. Prescott. "Rules Rather than Discretion: The Inconsistency of Optimal Plans." *The Journal of Political Economy*, Vol. 85, No. 3, 1977.

Lapin, Andrew. "Dempsey Maps Sequestration Cuts at Defense." *Government Executive*, June 19, 2012.

Larrabee, Eric. *Commander in Chief*. New York: Harper and Row, 1987.

Leavett, Harold J. *Top Down: Why Hierarchies are Here to Stay and How to Manage Them More Effectively*. Boston, MA: Harvard Business School Press, 2005.

Leed, Maren and David Sokolow. "The Ingenuity Gap: Officer Management for the 21st Century." Washington, DC: Center for Strategic and International Studies, International Security Program, January 2010.

Linebaugh, Kate. "The New GE Way: Go Deep, Not Wide." *The Wall Street Journal*, March 7, 2012.

Lowe, Janet C. *Warren Buffet Speaks: Wit and Wisdom from the World's Greatest Investor.* New York: John Wiley and Sons, Inc., 1997.

Maciariello, Joseph and Karen E. Linkletter. *Drucker's Lost Art of Management.* New York: McGraw Hill, 2011.

MacFarland, Sean, USA Brigadier General, Deputy Commandant, Army Command and General Staff College, Statement to the Subcommittee on Oversight and Investigations of the House Armed Services Committee, November 30, 2010.

Mahler, Walter H. *The Succession Planning Handbook for the Human Resource Executive.* Midland Park, NJ: Mahler Publishing Company, 1986.

Malone, Thomas W. *The Future of Work.* Boston, MA: Harvard Business School Press, 2004.

Markel, M. Wade. "The Limits of American Generalship: The JCS's Strategic Advice in Early Cold War Cases." *Parameters*, Spring 2008.

_____. "The Organization Man at War: Promotion Policies and Military Leadership, 1929-1992." Dissertation. Cambridge, MA: Harvard University, Department of History, 2000.

_____. "Winning Our Own Hearts and Minds: Promotion in Wartime." *Military Review*, November-December 2004.

Masland John W. and Laurence I. Radway. *Soldiers and Scholars: Military Education and National Policy*. Princeton, NJ: Princeton University Press, 1957.

Matthews, Lloyd. "The Uniformed Intellectual and his Place in American Arms." *Army Magazine*, August 2002.

McHugh, John M., Assistant Secretary of the Army (Manpower and Reserve Affairs). "Memo: Human Capital Management Reform." June 20, 2011.

McLeskey, James J. III. "The U.S. Army Professional Development of Officers Study: A Critique." Carlisle, PA: U.S. Army War College, March 22, 1986.

Meese, Michael and Samuel Calkins. "Back to the Future: Transforming the Army Officer Development System."*The Forum:* Vol. 4, No. 1, Art. 3. 2006.

Naylor, Sean D. "How To Fix My Army." *The Army Times,* July 8, 2002.

Nelson Jr., Otto L. "National Security and the General Staff." Washington, DC: *Infantry Journal Press*, 1946.

Oh, Paul S. and David E. Lewis. "Management and Leadership Performance in the Defense Department: Evidence from Surveys of Federal Employees." *Armed Forces & Society*, Vol. 34, No. 4, July 2008.

Oyos, Matthew M. "Theodore Roosevelt, Congress and the Military: US Civil-Military Relations in the Early Twentieth Century." *Presidential Studies Quarterly*, Vol. 30, No. 2, June 2000.

Peck, Don. "Can the Middle Class Be Saved?" *The Atlantic*, September 2011.

Pecoraro, Robert E. "George Catlett Marshall, Father of the United States Air Force: His Contributions to Air Power." U.S. Army War College Strategy Research Project, Carlisle, PA: U.S. Army War College, March 10, 2001.

Petraeus, David H. "Beyond the Cloister." *The American Interest*, July/August 2007, available from *www.the-american-interest.com/article.cfm?piece=290*.

"Plugged in HR: the General Electric Strategy." *HCA Online*, March 12, 2003.

Pogue, Forrest C. *George C. Marshall: Ordeal and Hope, 1939-1942*. New York: Viking Press, 1974.

Rajan, Raghuram G. and Julie Wulf. *The Flattening Firm: Evidence from Panel Data on the Changing Nature of Corporate Hierarchies*. National Bureau of Economic Research Working Paper No. 9633, Cambridge, MA: National Bureau of Economic Research, April 2003.

Reed, George E. "What's Wrong and What's Right with the War Colleges." *DefensePolicy.org*, July 1, 2011, available from *www.defensepolicy.org/2011/george-reed/what%E2%80%99s-wrong-and-right-with-the-war-colleges*.

Reingold, Jennifer. "CEO Swap: The $79 billion Plan." *CNN Money*, November 20, 2009.

Riley, Ryan *et al*. "2011 Center for Army Leadership Annual Survey of Army Leadership (CASAL): Main Findings." Fort Leavenworth, KS: Center for Army Leadership, Leadership Research, Assessment and Doctrine Division, May, 2012.

Rockefeller, Jay and Michael Chertoff. "A New Line of Defense in Cybersecurity." *Washington Post*, November 18, 2011.

Rodriguez, Robert. "Coming to an Office Near You: HR Professionals with Wide-Ranging Business Skills and a Desire for Challenging Work." *HR Magazine*, Vol. 51, No. 1, March 1, 2006.

Rosen, Sherwin. "The Military as an Internal Labor Market: Some Allocation, Productivity, and Incentive Problems." *Social Science Quarterly*, Vol. 73, No. 2, June 1992.

Saari, Lise M. *et al*. "A Survey of Management Training and Education Practices in U.S. Companies." *Personnel Psychology*, Vol. 41, 1988.

Sarkesian, Sam C. and William J. Taylor, Jr. "The Case for Civilian Graduate Education for Professional Officers." *Armed Forces & Society*, January 1, 1975.

Scales, Robert H. "Too Busy to Learn." *U.S. Naval Institute Proceedings*, February 2010.

Schifferle, Peter J. *America's School for War*, Lawrence, KS: University of Kansas Press, 2010.

Schirmer, Peter *et al.* "Challenging Time in DOPMA." Santa Monica, CA: RAND National Defense Research Institute, 2006.

Schultz, Theodore W. "Investments in Human Capital." *American Economic Review*, Vol. 51, No. 1, March 1961.

_____. "The Value of the Ability to Deal with Disequilibria." *Journal of Economic Literature*, Vol. 13, No. 3, September 1975.

Sisson, E. Donald. "Forced Choice: The New Army Ratings." *Personnel Psychology*, Vol. 1, No. 3, Autumn 1948.

Slater, Robert. *Get Better or Get Beaten: 29 Leadership Secrets from Jack Welch*. New York: McGraw-Hill, 2001.

Snow, Donald P. "The Golden Age, Vignettes of Military History." No. 92. Carlisle, PA: U.S. Army Military History Institute, March 6, 1978.

Sorley, Lewis, ed. *Press On: Selected Works of General Don A. Starry*. Fort Leavenworth: Combat Institute Press, 2009.

Sorley, Lewis. "The Will-o'-the-Wisp General." Paper presented at the National Conference of the Inter-University Seminar on Armed Forces and Society, Chicago, IL. October 25, 1980.

Spence, Michael. "Signaling in Retrospect and the Informational Structure of Markets," Nobel Prize lecture, December 8, 2001.

_____. "Job Market Signaling." *The Quarterly Journal of Economics*, Vol. 87, No. 3, August 1973.

"A Statement on the Posture of the United States Army 2011." 1st Sess., 112th Cong., March 2011.

Stavnes, Robert P. "Is the Army's Current Force Management System Working?" Carlisle, PA: U.S. Army War College, March 15, 2008.

Steele, William. "Training and Developing Leaders in a Transforming Army." *Military Review*, September-October, 2001.

Stiglitz, Joseph E. and Linda J. Bilmes, "The True Cost of the Iraq War: $3 Trillion and Beyond," *The Washington Post*, September 5, 2010.

Stringer, Kevin. "Distilling the Demographic Dividend: Retaining U.S. Army Officer Talent for the 40-year Career?" *The Land Warfare Papers*, No. 89, June 2012.

_____. "The War on Terror and the War for Officer Talent: Linked Challenges for the U.S. Army." Arlington, VA: Association of the United States Army, July 2008.

Taylor, Frederick Winslow. *The Principles of Scientific Management*. New York: Harper and Brothers, 1911.

Tulgan, Bruce. *Winning the Talent Wars*. New York: W. W. Norton & Co., 2001.

Tversky, Amos and Daniel Kahneman. "Judgment under Uncertainty: Heuristics and Biases." *Science*, Vol. 185, No. 4157, September 27, 1974.

U.S. Army Deputy Chief of Staff, G3/5/7, "Army Leaders for the 21st Century." Washington, DC: Department of the Army, November, 2006.

U.S. Army 2025: Title X Challenges. Washington, DC: U.S. Army Directed Studies Office, Western Hemisphere Branch.

U.S. Army Business Transformation Plan 2011, Washington, DC: U.S. Army Office of Business Transformation. October 1, 2010.

U.S. Army A Leader Development Strategy for a 21st Century Army. Washington, DC: U.S. Army Training and Doctrine Command, November 25, 2009.

U.S. Army Pamphlet 525-3-0: "The Army Capstone Concept. Operational Adaptability: Operating under Conditions of Uncertainty and Complexity in an era of Persistent Conflict, 2016-2028. Washington, DC: U.S. Army Training and Doctrine Command, December 21, 2009.

U.S. Army Pamphlet 523-3-7: "The U.S. Army Concept for the Human Dimension in Full Spectrum Operations, 2015-2024. Washington, DC: U.S. Army Training and Doctrine Command, June 11, 2008.

U.S. Army Training and Doctrine Command. "The Profession of Arms: An Army White Paper." Washington, DC: U.S. Army Training and Doctrine Command. December 2, 2010.

U.S. Army Officer Study Report to the Army. Washington, DC: U.S. Army Training and Leader Development Panel, 2001.

U.S. Army Strategic Leadership Primer, 3rd Ed. Carlisle, PA: Department of Command, Leadership, and Management, U.S. Army War College, 2010.

U.S. Department of Defense *Instruction 1320.14: Commissioned Officer Promotion Program Procedures*, Washington, DC: U.S. Department of Defense, September 24, 1996.

U.S. Department of Defense. *Capstone Concept for Joint Operations*, Version 3.0, Washington, DC: U.S. Department of Defense, January 15, 2009.

U.S. Department of Defense. *National Defense Strategy*, Washington, DC: U.S. Department of Defense, June 2008.

U.S. Department of Defense. *Sustaining U.S. Global Leadership: Priorities for 21st Century Defense*, Washington, DC: U.S. Department of Defense, January, 2012.

U.S. Department of Defense. *Quadrennial Defense Review Report*, Washington, DC: U.S. Department of Defense, February 6, 2006.

U.S. Government Accountability Office. *Results-Oriented Cultures: Implementation Steps to Assist Mergers and Organizational Transformations*, GAO-03-669, Washington, DC: U.S. Government Accountability Office, July 2003.

U.S. Government Accountability Office. *Strategic Plan Needed to Address Army's Emerging Officer Accession and Retention Challenges*, GAO-07-224, Washington, DC: U.S. Government Accountability Office, January 2007.

U.S. House of Representatives, Committee on Armed Services (Subcommittee on Oversight and Investigations). "Another Crossroads? Professional Military Education Two Decades after the Goldwater Nichols Act and the Skelton Panel," Washington, DC, April 2010.

U.S. Joint Chiefs of Staff. *The National Military Strategy of the United States of America 2011: Redefining America's Military Leadership*, Washington , DC: U.S. Joint Chiefs of Staff, February 8, 2011.

U.S. Joint Forces Command. *2010 Joint Operating Environment*. Norfolk, VA: U.S. Joint Forces Command.

U.S. War Department. *General Orders No. 57*, Washington, DC: U.S. War Department, 1942.

U.S. War Department. *Report on Educational System for Officers of the Army*, Washington, DC: U.S. War Department, Military Education Board, May 27, 1945.

Vandergriff, Donald E. "Culture Wars," in Robert Bateman, ed., *Digital War: A View from the Frontline*, New York: IBooks, Inc., July 29, 2003.

_____. "One Step Forward, Two Steps Back: Mission Command versus the Army Personnel System." *The Land Warfare Papers*, No. 84, August, 2011.

Vosburgh, Richard M. "The Evolution of HR: Developing HR as an Internal Consulting Organization." *Human Resource Planning Journal* Vol. 30, No. 3, September 2007.

Wardynski, Casey, David S. Lyle, and Michael J. Colarusso. "Towards a U.S. Army Officer Corps Strategy for Success: A Proposed Human Capital Model Focused Upon Talent." Carlisle, PA: Strategic Studies Institute, U.S. Army War College, April 2009.

_____. "Talent: Implications for a U.S. Army Officer Corps Strategy." Carlisle, PA: Strategic Studies Institute, U.S. Army War College, November 2009.

_____. "Towards a U.S. Army Officer Corps Strategy for Success: Retaining Talent." Carlisle, PA: Strategic Studies Institute, U.S. Army War College, January 2010.

_____. "Accessing Talent: The Foundation of a U.S. Army Officer Corps Strategy." Carlisle, PA: Strategic Studies Institute, U.S. Army War College, February 2010.

_____. "Towards a U.S. Army Officer Corps Strategy for Success: Developing Talent." Carlisle, PA: Strategic Studies Institute, U.S. Army War College, March 2010.

_____. "Towards a U.S. Army Officer Corps Strategy for Success: Employing Talent." Carlisle, PA: Strategic Studies Institute, U.S. Army War College, May 2010.

Whyte, William H. *The Organization Man*. New York: Doubleday, 1956.

Wong, Leonard. "Generations Apart: Xers and Boomers in the Officer Corps." Carlisle, PA: Strategic Studies Institute, U.S. Army War College, 2000.

ABOUT THE AUTHORS

MICHAEL J. COLARUSSO is a senior research analyst in the Army's Office of Economic and Manpower Analysis at the United States Military Academy, West Point. U.S. Army Lieutenant Colonel (Retired) Colarusso co-authored the six-monograph "Officer Talent Management Series" published by the Strategic Studies Institute, U.S. Army War College. His primary areas of research are organizational design, generational dynamics, human capital and talent management. Lieutenant Colonel (Retired) Colarusso holds a B.A. in history from Saint John's University and an M.A. in history from the Pennsylvania State University.

DAVID S. LYLE is an Associate Professor of Economics and Director of the Army's Office of Economic and Manpower Analysis at the United States Military Academy, West Point, NY. U.S. Army Lieutenant Colonel Lyle co-authored the six-monograph "Officer Talent Management Series" published by the Strategic Studies Institute, U.S. Army War College. His primary areas of research are labor economics, econometrics, human capital, and talent management. Lieutenant Colonel Lyle holds a B.S. from West Point and a Ph.D. in economics from the Massachusetts Institute of Technology.

U.S. ARMY WAR COLLEGE

Major General Anthony A. Cucolo III
Commandant

*****

STRATEGIC STUDIES INSTITUTE
and
U.S. ARMY WAR COLLEGE PRESS

Director
Professor Douglas C. Lovelace, Jr.

Director of Research
Dr. Steven K. Metz

Authors
Lieutenant Colonel Michael J. Colarusso,
U.S. Army (Retired)
Lieutenant Colonel David S. Lyle

Editor for Production
Dr. James G. Pierce

Publications Assistant
Ms. Rita A. Rummel

*****

Composition
Mrs. Jennifer E. Nevil

www.ingramcontent.com/pod-product-compliance
Lightning Source LLC
Chambersburg PA
CBHW080541170426
43195CB00016B/2641